Teens and Substance Abuse

Peggy J. Parks

Teen Well-Being

ReferencePoint
Press®

San Diego, CA

For more information, contact:
ReferencePoint Press, Inc.
PO Box 27779
San Diego, CA 92198
www.ReferencePointPress.com

Picture credits:
Cover: Thinkstock Images
Depositphotos, 11
Thinkstock Images, 15
Steve Zmina, 30, 31, 32, 33, 45, 45, 59, 60, 61, 73, 74, 75

LIBRARY OF CONGRESS CATALOGING-IN-PUBLICATION DATA

Parks, Peggy J., 1951–
  Teens and substance abuse / by Peggy J. Parks.
    pages cm. -- (Compact research series)
  Includes bibliographical references and index.
   ISBN 978-1-60152-832-2 (hardback) -- ISBN 1-60152-832-9 (hardback) 1. Teenagers--
Substance use--Juvenile literature. 2. Teenagers--Drug use--Juvenile literature. 3. Substance
abuse--Juvenile literature. I. Title.
  HV4999.Y68P37   2016
  362.290835--dc23

                                     2015007513

Contents

Foreword

As modern civilization continues to evolve, its ability to create, store, distribute, and access information expands exponentially. The explosion of information from all media continues to increase at a phenomenal rate. By 2020 some experts predict the worldwide information base will double every seventy-three days. While access to diverse sources of information and perspectives is paramount to any democratic society, information alone cannot help people gain knowledge and understanding. Information must be organized and presented clearly and succinctly in order to be understood. The challenge in the digital age becomes not the creation of information, but how best to sort, organize, enhance, and present information.

ReferencePoint Press developed the *Compact Research* series with this challenge of the information age in mind. More than any other subject area today, researching current issues can yield vast, diverse, and unqualified information that can be intimidating and overwhelming for even the most advanced and motivated researcher. The *Compact Research* series offers a compact, relevant, intelligent, and conveniently organized collection of information covering a variety of current topics ranging from illegal immigration and deforestation to diseases such as anorexia and meningitis.

The series focuses on three types of information: objective single-author narratives, opinion-based primary source quotations, and facts and statistics. The clearly written objective narratives provide context and reliable background information. Primary source quotes are carefully selected and cited, exposing the reader to differing points of view, and facts and statistics sections aid the reader in evaluating perspectives. Presenting these key types of information creates a richer, more balanced learning experience.

For better understanding and convenience, the series enhances information by organizing it into narrower topics and adding design features that make it easy for a reader to identify desired content. For example, in *Compact Research: Illegal Immigration*, a chapter covering the economic impact of illegal immigration has an objective narrative explaining the various ways the economy is impacted, a balanced section of numerous primary source quotes on the topic, followed by facts and full-color illustrations to encourage evaluation of contrasting perspectives.

The ancient Roman philosopher Lucius Annaeus Seneca wrote, "It is quality rather than quantity that matters." More than just a collection of content, the *Compact Research* series is simply committed to creating, finding, organizing, and presenting the most relevant and appropriate amount of information on a current topic in a user-friendly style that invites, intrigues, and fosters understanding.

Teen Substance Abuse at a Glance

Types of Substances Abused by Teens

Alcohol, marijuana, MDMA (also known as Molly), synthetic drugs, steroids, prescription drugs, and a host of other substances are abused by teens.

Scope of the Problem

A major survey conducted in 2014 shows that more than one-fourth of teenagers had used some type of illicit drug, and 41 percent drank alcohol on an annual basis.

How Teens Get Alcohol and Drugs

Surveys show that it is not difficult for teens to get alcohol and drugs, and the substances are usually obtained from friends, relatives, or acquaintances.

Online Sellers

By accessing hidden websites teens can order most any drug they want from online sellers.

Warning Signs

Symptoms of substance abuse range from personality changes and loss of interest in favorite activities to academic decline, poor health, and relationship problems with friends and family.

Why Teens Abuse Alcohol and Drugs

Contributing factors include peer pressure, stress, lack of perceived harm, and poor decision making, the latter of which is due to adolescent brains not yet being fully developed.

Consequences

From alcohol poisoning to brain damage and death from overdose, teens who drink and do drugs put their health and well-being in danger.

Treatment Options

Many different avenues are open to those who need to be treated for substance abuse, but only about 10 percent of teens ever seek treatment.

Addressing the Problem

Education and awareness programs can help teens understand the risks involved with substance abuse and learn how to avoid alcohol and drugs.

Overview

"Alcohol and other drug use among our nation's youth remains a major public health problem."

—Centers for Disease Control and Prevention (CDC), whose mission is to protect the United States from health and safety threats, both foreign and domestic.

"Virtually every drug that is abused by adults is also abused by adolescents."

—Roxanne Dryden-Edwards, an adult, child, and adolescent psychiatrist from Gaithersburg, Maryland.

When Taylor Snider was seventeen years old, she took drugs for the first time in her life—and nearly died from it. While growing up in Vancouver, British Columbia, Snider never had any interest in drugs. Then during the summer of 2014 her friends encouraged her to try something they called Molly. After several weekends of watching them take the pills and saying no when they asked her to join them, Snider finally gave in and took the drug. Within an hour she was violently ill and vomited throughout the night. In the morning she started having seizures and was rushed to the hospital where she lapsed into a coma. Her condition was grave. "The only way they could tell I was alive is because my heart was beating and I was breathing,"[1] she says. When her parents arrived at the hospital, they received devastating news: Their daughter might never wake up.

Snider remained in the coma for forty-six hours and then came out of it. She woke up confused and frightened because she had no memory of what had happened. "Unaware of where I was or why I was there, I began to panic,"[2] she says. Snider could not understand why her parents were sitting by her bedside with tears streaming down their faces, and they explained how close she came to dying. Because of her terrifying experience, Snider has strong words for other young people who might consider experimenting with Molly. "Taking the drug is like playing Russian roulette with your body. . . . If you don't want this to happen to you, or put your family through this, simply don't take the chance."[3]

The Molly Story

Molly is one of the nicknames for a drug whose chemical name is 3,4-methylenedioxy-methamphetamine, or MDMA for short. Although not all teens die or come close to dying from taking it, the risk is always there. Also called X and Ecstasy (Mandy in the United Kingdom), Molly's effect is to release excessive amounts of brain chemicals known as neurotransmitters; specifically, the mood-altering neurotransmitters dopamine, serotonin, and norepinephrine. A Columbia University health site explains: "Ecstasy prevents the 'recycling' of these neurotransmitters by the brain while also encouraging the release of more. Thus, the brain is essentially flooded, especially with serotonin. The effect may last several hours, though the substance is still being metabolized long after the high has worn off."[4]

MDMA was originally created in 1912 by the pharmaceutical company Merck. The drug remained largely unknown until the mid-1970s when it came to the attention of chemist Alexander Shulgin. In 1976 he synthesized MDMA in his home laboratory in Lafayette, California, and then tested it on himself. Pleased with its effects and believing the drug had therapeutic promise, Shulgin started giving samples to therapists for use with their patients. He never intended for MDMA to become a mainstream drug—but once people experienced its euphoric effects, demand began to soar. By the 1980s MDMA had been dubbed "Ecstasy," and clandestine laboratories were manufacturing and selling it.

One claim Molly users often make is that it is pure rather than mixed

> " One claim Molly fans often make is that it is pure, rather than mixed (or cut) with other substances, but that is a myth. "

(or cut) with other substances, but that is a myth. "Just because it says Molly on the label, that means nothing," says Rusty Payne of the US Drug Enforcement Administration (DEA). "Molly can be whatever the drug dealer wants it to be."[5] According to the DEA only 13 percent of the Molly seized in New York since 2009 contained any MDMA at all. Drugs being touted as "pure" MDMA have been found to contain substances such as methamphetamine, cocaine, talcum powder, heroin, and LSD—as well as pesticides and rat poison. When teens take Molly they have absolutely no idea what is in it, who made it, or whether it was created in a basement lab in Texas or a garage in Taiwan.

Abundant Choices

Molly has garnered a great deal of publicity in recent years, but it is just one of many substances teens use to get high. Aside from alcohol (the most popular of all substances), teens also abuse prescription drugs, especially painkillers such as hydrocodone (Vicodin) and oxycodone (OxyContin). Performance-enhancing drugs such as anabolic steroids, which are synthetic variants of the naturally occurring male hormone testosterone, are abused by thousands of teens each year. Then there are the inhalants, which are common household products that contain volatile solvents or aerosols. National Institute on Drug Abuse (NIDA) director Nora D. Volkow describes some of the substances that teens inhale in a practice known as huffing: "Products such as glues, nail polish remover, lighter fluid, spray paints, deodorant and hair sprays, whipped cream canisters, and cleaning fluids are widely available yet far from innocuous. Many young people inhale the vapors from these sources in search of quick intoxication."[6]

A variety of illegal drugs are used by teens, the most common of which is marijuana (usually called pot or weed). Others are stimulants like amphetamines, cocaine, and methamphetamine (meth); hallucinogens such as LSD and mushrooms; heroin; and MDMA. Synthetic drugs are packaged and sold under deceptive names that are intended to escape detection by law enforcement. "These insidious substances are often marketed directly to teenagers and young adults as a 'legal' alternative to other illicit substances such as marijuana," says DEA administrator Michele Leonhart. "In reality, they are incredibly dangerous."[7]

The synthetic drug colloquially called "bath salts" has nothing to do with bathing; rather, it is a synthetic stimulant that contains powerful

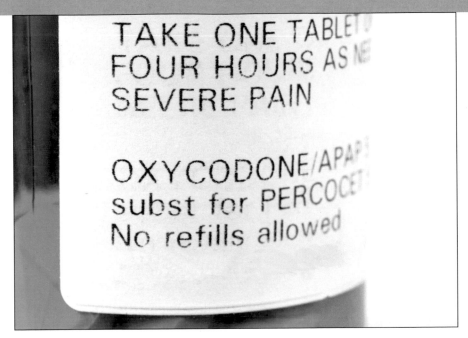

Today's teens use a wide variety of substances for getting high. Alcohol is still the most popular substance of choice, but prescription drugs (especially painkillers such as oxycodone), marijuana (natural and synthetic), heroin, and MDMA are among the drugs that are abused by teens.

psychoactive chemicals known as cathinones. The drug sold as Spice, K2, or Black Mamba is often called synthetic marijuana (cannabis) or "fake pot" because it looks something like marijuana. It is not at all the same, however. Synthetic cannabis consists of dried, shredded plant material that has been sprayed with chemicals such as cannabinoids, which are synthetic versions of the psychoactive ingredient in marijuana, tetrahydrocannabinol (THC). Experts say the synthetic drug is at least one hundred times more powerful than natural THC. "You would think it would be safe, would be OK, it's an alternative to marijuana, and it's anything but that," says Devin Eckhardt, whose son Connor died in July 2014 after taking just one hit of Spice. "It's a deadly poison."[8]

How Serious a Problem Is Substance Abuse Among Teens?

To keep a close watch on substance abuse trends among teenagers in the United States, the NIDA sponsors an annual study called Monitoring the Future (MTF). The survey involves students in eighth, tenth, and twelfth grades who attend public and private schools throughout the country. More than forty-one thousand teens were involved in the 2014 survey, which was published in February 2015. NIDA officials were encouraged by the findings because, as the agency explains, they showed "decreasing use of alcohol, cigarettes, and prescription pain relievers; no increase in use of marijuana; decreasing use of inhalants and synthetic drugs, including K2/Spice and bath salts; and a general decline over the last two decades in the use of illicit drugs."[9]

> " Pot smoking teens find it difficult to focus and pay attention and may appear lethargic, spending hours just staring at the ceiling. "

The decline in current alcohol use among teens was another area of improvement. During the 2014 survey 22.6 percent of teens said they drank alcohol during the past thirty days, compared with nearly 40 percent in 1991. Binge drinking, which is defined as five or more drinks in a row, also declined. The survey showed that 19.4 percent of high school seniors reported binge drinking in 2014, compared with 31.5 percent in 1998. Findings about marijuana were mixed. Although the NIDA was encouraged to see that use of the drug had remained roughly the same since 2010, current marijuana use was significantly higher for all three grades than in 1991 and 1992.

Red Flags

Warning signs of substance abuse can differ widely from teen to teen depending on a variety of factors, but the NIDA offers some general thoughts about symptoms: "If an adolescent starts behaving differently for no apparent reason—such as acting withdrawn, frequently tired or depressed, or hostile—it could be a sign he or she is developing a drug-related problem. Parents and others may overlook such signs, believing them to be a normal part of puberty."[10] Other possible warning signs include a sudden change in friendships and peer groups, noticeable changes in eating or sleeping habits, a loss of interest in favorite hobbies or activities, and a decline in academic performance, often linked with missing classes or skipping school.

Teens who regularly smoke marijuana often exhibit a number of obvious signs. "A few are the kind of stereotypical behavior often seen in movies and on TV," says an August 2013 article by health writer Suzanne Kane, "while others point to a pattern of behavior that is more disturbing."[11] Signs of regular pot use include frequent cravings for junk food, laughter at inappropriate moments, and chronically red eyes with frequent use of eye drops. Pot smoking teens find it difficult to focus and pay attention and may appear lethargic, spending hours just staring at the ceiling. One of the most obvious signs is small burns on the thumb and forefinger. "This is caused by smoking a joint down to the end," says Kane. "It isn't from a science experiment at school."[12]

Where Do Teens Get Alcohol and Drugs?

Research has consistently shown that it is not difficult for teens to get alcohol and drugs. This is especially true of alcohol, a fact that was revealed in a 2014 survey by the CDC. The survey involved more than thirteen thousand high school students. Of those who recently drank alcohol, nearly 42 percent said someone had given it to them. "They get it from friends or family members, at parties, or by taking it without permission," notes a 2013 report by the Federal Trade Commission. "Underage drinkers who pay for alcohol usually give money to someone else to buy it."[13]

Marijuana, Molly, and many other illicit substances are also easy for teens to get. During the 2014 MTF survey, 81 percent of high school seniors said they could easily get marijuana if they wanted to. During a 2012 survey by the National Center on Addiction and Substance Abuse at Columbia University (CASAColumbia), nearly half of teen respondents said they knew someone who sold drugs at their school, including marijuana, prescription drugs, cocaine, and Molly.

The Dark Web

One fact that is highly disturbing to parents, substance abuse professionals, and law enforcement is that teens can order drugs from websites. Secretive online marketplaces, collectively referred to as the Dark Web (or Dark Net), are tucked away in hidden spots on the Internet. They are known to sell everything from marijuana, Molly, heroin, meth, and synthetic drugs to just about any prescription medicine. The sites cannot be found by Google or other search engines; they are only accessible to those who know about them and use special browser software to access them.

One of these sites, an expansive underground emporium called Silk Road, was created in 2011 by Ross Ulbricht, whose screen name was Dread Pirate Roberts. Ulbricht sold everything from a staggering array of drugs to illegal firearms. Journalist Carole Cadwalladr was able to log onto the Silk Road site while working on an investigative story. She says it was like "stumbling into a parallel universe, a universe where eBay had been taken over by international drug cartels and Amazon offers a choice of books, DVDS and hallucinogens."[14] In October 2013 Ulbricht was arrested by the FBI, and Silk Road was shut down. He was later convicted on seven federal charges and as of February 2015 was facing a prison sentence of thirty years to life.

> " Secretive online marketplaces, collectively referred to as the Dark Web (or Dark Net), are tucked away in hidden spots on the Internet. "

Why Do Teens Abuse Alcohol and Drugs?

What compels young people to drink alcohol or use drugs is a complex issue, one that is difficult even for experts to fully understand. Most psychologists believe there are numerous reasons. "Various factors can contribute to teen drug abuse, from insecurity to a desire for social acceptance," explains the Mayo Clinic. "Teens often feel indestructible and might not consider the consequences of their actions, leading them to take dangerous risks—such as abusing legal or illegal drugs."[15]

One of the top reasons teens give when asked why they started taking drugs is peer pressure: the strong desire to be liked and feel included. This was the case with a young man named Will, whose family moved to Ohio from their home in Virginia when he was fifteen. Will felt out of place in his new environment. "I felt like I really didn't fit in," he says. "I didn't know who I was. I began to use drugs to fit into a certain group and feel accepted among that group. I was kind of lost. That was a way of finding myself."[16]

Influential Social Media

In recent years the popularity of social media sites such as Facebook, Tumblr, and Pinterest, and social media apps such as Instagram and Twitter, has soared. This concerns substance abuse experts because exposure to pictures and posts about drinking and drug abuse can influence teens to drink and take drugs. During the August 2012 CASAColumbia survey, 75 percent of teens said that seeing pictures of kids partying with alcohol and marijuana encourages other teens to want to party like that. The study shows that teens who had seen such pictures were four times likelier to have used marijuana and more than three times likelier to have used alcohol.

From May to December 2013 researchers from the Washington University School of Medicine conducted a study to assess the influence of pro-marijuana tweets on young people. Their focus was on a Twitter user whose screen name (or handle) was @stillblazingtho. At the time of the study he/she had approximately 1 million followers, of whom nearly three-fourths were nineteen or younger. An analysis of several thousand tweets by the followers reveals that they were heavily influenced by the pro-pot remarks tweeted by @stillblazingtho: Their tweets showed

> One of the top reasons teens give when asked why they started taking drugs is peer pressure: the strong desire to be liked and feel included.

overwhelmingly positive thoughts about marijuana and very little perception of risk. In the final report, the study authors write: "Young people are especially responsive to social media influences and often establish substance use patterns during this phase of development. Our findings underscore the need for surveillance efforts to monitor the pro-marijuana content reaching young people on Twitter."[17]

What Are the Consequences of Substance Abuse?

The consequences for young people who drink alcohol and/or take drugs range from relatively minor (a hangover from drinking) to severe (lasting brain damage or death from toxic drugs). The wide range of risks is em-

Images that show teenagers partying with alcohol and marijuana are often posted on social media sites. These images, and the comments that go with them, can influence other teens to do the same.

phasized in a September 2013 paper by the nonpartisan research group Child Trends. The paper addresses the effects of drugs such as marijuana, prescription drugs, inhalants, and hallucinogens. "Use of illicit drugs is associated with many harmful behaviors," the authors explain, "and can cause both short- and long-term health problems." They continue:

> Adolescents who use illicit drugs are more likely than other adolescents to engage in risky sexual behavior, or be involved in delinquency and crime. Additionally, students using illicit drugs often have problems in school, although it is not easy to determine which comes first—the drug use, or the school problems. These school problems include low attendance, poor academic perfor-

mance, and a greater likelihood of dropping out or being expelled. Furthermore, illicit drug use can affect relationships with family and friends by causing adolescents to be unreliable, forgetful, dishonest, or violent.[18]

Substance Abuse Treatment for Teens

Once young people are able/ready to admit that they have a substance abuse problem and need help, many options are available to them. Recommended treatment plans vary depending on the individual and his or her needs. "Whatever a person's age," says the NIDA, "treatment is not 'one size fits all.' It requires taking into account the needs of the whole person—including his or her developmental stage and cognitive abilities and the influence of family, friends, and others in the person's life, as well as any additional mental or physical health conditions."[19] Teens who are treated for substance abuse typically undergo one or more types of therapy, as well as participate in peer support groups to help encourage abstinence and prevent relapse.

> Once young people are able/ready to admit that they have a substance abuse problem and need help, many options are available to them.

The day before Nick Gerl turned fifteen, his parents admitted him to an adolescent residential treatment facility in Houston, Texas. Gerl had started smoking pot when he was twelve and went on to habitually abuse prescription drugs. Although he knew he was addicted to drugs, Gerl did not want to go to the treatment center and tried to escape twice while he was a patient there. He made it through the program, though, and after just over seven months of treatment, he was able to go home. "My family life is a lot better," he says. "I'm realizing there are fun things in life that I can do sober. I got a chance to get clean and I have my whole life ahead of me."[20]

What Can Be Done About Teen Substance Abuse?

Because of the complexity of the teen substance abuse problem, experts recommend a combination of strategies. "Many factors and strategies can help adolescents stay drug free," says the Office of Adolescent Health. "Strong positive connections with parents, other family members, school, and religion; having parents present clear limits and consistent enforcement of discipline; and reduced access in the home to illegal substances."[21]

> Teen substance abuse is not a new problem, nor is it something for which there is a quick-fix solution.

Among the most powerful, impactful methods of getting through to teens about alcohol and drugs are speaker programs. Teens and/or parents visit schools and talk frankly to students about personal tragedies. This was how Steve Flannigan coped with the death of his daughter, Brittany, who died after taking Molly in August 2014. Overwhelmed by grief, Flannigan decided to do something to save other teens, and he began sharing Brittany's story at schools and colleges. After hearing his presentation at a Boston, Massachusetts, college, the students were stunned into silence. They had heard plenty of warnings about drinking and drugs, but none had resonated with them like this one. Twenty-year-old Erin Bruce commented: "To hear your story firsthand, for you to say, 'This was my daughter, and you know she did everything right except for this one thing' . . . it's heavy."[22]

Looking Ahead

Teen substance abuse is not a new problem, nor is it something for which there is a quick-fix solution. Thousands of young people continue to use alcohol and drugs, and they have innumerable reasons for doing so. Convincing them to stop, or never start in the first place, is a formidable task. Yet education and prevention strategies may be making a difference because certain forms of substance abuse have declined or are tapering off. Health officials hope to build on that momentum in the coming years.

How Serious a Problem Is Substance Abuse Among Teens?

"For millions of teens, high school is a convenient place to get high; for millions of parents trying to raise drug-free kids, the 'high' school years are the most dangerous time their children face."

—Joseph A. Califano Jr., founder and former chairman of the National Center on Addiction and Substance Abuse at Columbia University.

"People see the kids who are outside of school, in the community and doing the drugs and alcohol. But there are more of us in school, doing the right thing that people don't see. There are more of us than them."

—Cassidy Hyde, a high school student from Elyria, Ohio.

Whether teen substance abuse is a big problem, a small problem, or something in between is largely based on opinion and interpretation of statistics. One fact cannot be denied, though: Thousands of young people throughout the United States drink alcohol and use a wide variety of drugs.

To keep track of fluctuations in teen substance abuse, researchers from the University of Michigan Institute for Social Justice interview tens of thousands of teens each year in the Monitoring the Future (MTF) survey. Says Lloyd D. Johnston, a research scientist who cofounded the

MTF program: "The study fills a need in society to know how things are changing, how fast they are changing, and, especially, whether new drugs are coming onto the scene." Johnston emphasizes why it is important to monitor teen substance abuse trends. "We've seen a growing smorgasbord of drugs come to the table, while very few have left," he says. "There will always be new drugs to tempt adolescents."[23]

Good News, Bad News

When the 2014 MTF survey was published in February 2015, it showed improvement in some areas and troubling trends in others. "There is a lot of good news in this year's results," says Johnston, "but the problems of teen substance use and abuse are still far from going away."[24] One drug whose popularity had not diminished with teens is marijuana. Although the number of high school seniors who recently smoked marijuana (21.2 percent) was slightly lower than 2012 and 2013, it was much higher than the 13.8 percent reported in 1991. Also revealed in the MTF survey was that from 1991 to 2014 use of marijuana by tenth graders nearly doubled, and use did double among eighth graders.

> " Whether teen substance abuse is a big problem, a small problem, or something in between is largely based on opinion and interpretation of statistics. "

Some findings from the 2014 youth survey were more encouraging. For instance, use of MDMA was shown to be declining. Although health officials remain concerned about the popularity of Molly among youth, 8 percent of teens were reportedly using it in 1996 (the first year it was included as a category), and the 2014 survey showed prevalence had declined to 3.5 percent. Inhalant use among teens had also declined. During the 1991 survey, 17 percent of students said they had engaged in huffing. That number grew to a peak of 19.4 percent in 1995, and by 2014 it had dipped below 9 percent.

Of all the substances evaluated during the MTF survey, alcohol use among teens seems to have decreased the most. Current alcohol use among high school seniors was found to be markedly lower than it had

been in years. In 1991, for instance, more than half of high school seniors admitted drinking alcohol in the past thirty days, and by 2014 the
number had dropped to 37.4 percent. Considerable declines in drinking
were also shown among younger students. The 2014 survey found that
only 9 percent of eighth graders drank alcohol at some point during the
past month, compared with 25 percent of that age group in 1991. An
even sharper decline in drinking was seen among tenth graders: Nearly
43 percent admitted drinking alcohol during the past month in 1991,
and by 2014 it had dropped to 23.5 percent.

Binge Drinking Among Teens

As promising as the significant decline in teen drinking is, health officials remain concerned about the thousands of young people who drink
alcohol. Of particular concern, because of the enormous risks involved,
is binge drinking, which is defined as five or more drinks in a row during
the past two weeks. "Binge drinking is the most common form of alcohol consumption among adolescents,"[25] says the research group Child
Trends, which found that nearly one
in four (22 percent) twelfth graders
reported this behavior in 2013.

> **One drug whose popularity has not diminished with teens is marijuana.**

The most excessive form of alcohol consumption in a short period of time is known as "extreme
binge drinking." This risky practice
is defined as having ten or more, or
fifteen or more, drinks in a row at
least once during the prior two weeks. The findings of a study released
in 2013 by public health researcher Megan Patrick reveal that while
binge drinking had slowed down considerably between 2005 and 2011,
extreme binge drinking declined only slightly. "The rates are alarming
when you think of a class of 30 students, that several kids in the class will
be drinking at very dangerous levels,"[26] says Patrick.

Campus Consumption

Colleges and universities throughout the United States struggle with
binge drinking among students. According to the National Institute
on Alcohol Abuse and Alcoholism (NIAAA), more than 80 percent of

college students drink alcohol; of those, almost half report recent binge drinking. "Drinking at college has become a ritual that students often see as an integral part of their higher-education experience," says the NIAAA. "Many students come to college with established drinking habits, and the college environment can exacerbate the problem."[27] A 2014 paper by NIAAA researchers Aaron White and Ralph Hingson found that unlike at high schools, there has been no downward trend in binge drinking at the college level; rather, drinking levels have stayed relatively stable over the past thirty years. According to White and Hingson, research has shown that roughly two out of five male and female college students engage in binge drinking.

One school that has long been known for its culture of heavy drinking is Dartmouth College in Hanover, New Hampshire. A 2015 report commissioned by Dartmouth officials shows that freshmen students who begin their studies at the prestigious Ivy League school are less likely than the national average to participate in high-risk drinking—but within just one year of being there, they become *more* likely to binge drink than the national average. As Dartmouth president Philip J. Hanlon has remarked, "Dangerous drinking has become the rule and not the exception."[28]

Designer Drugs

For numerous reasons synthetic drugs pose some of the most complicated, challenging problems related to teen substance abuse. Also called designer drugs, synthetic cannabis (Spice and K2) and cathinones (bath salts) were not included in any youth substance abuse studies until 2012 because they were virtually unheard of. Today, health care providers and law enforcement officials are alarmed at how fast the drugs' popularity—and use—has grown. According to the NIDA, synthetic cannabis is extremely popular among high school seniors, second only to natural marijuana. "Easy access and the misperception that Spice products are 'natural' and therefore harmless have likely contributed to their popularity," writes the NIDA. "Another selling point is that the chemicals used in Spice are not easily detected in standard drug tests."[29]

By "easy access" the NIDA is referring to the availability of synthetic cannabis compared with other illicit drugs. Although law enforcement has clamped down on the sale of designer drugs, these are still often sold openly in convenience stores, gas stations, and tobacco shops. This is extremely difficult to stop because the drugs are often made in China and other countries that do not have strict rules about drugs or the chemicals used to make them. As soon as certain compounds are added to state or federal lists of illegal substances, manufacturers simply tweak the formulas so they are no longer technically illegal. "Brand new chemicals are constantly being synthesized and entering the market," says Karen Dobner, whose teenage son Max died after smoking synthetic pot. "These chemicals have never been seen on Earth before. So, basically our young people are acting as lab rats, and the experiment isn't going well at all."[30]

A situation in December 2013 illustrates how synthetic drug manufacturers are able to skirt the law. While working on an investigative story journalist Eliza Gray visited an Amarillo, Texas, novelty shop called Planet X. Police had previously raided the shop and confiscated more than ninety packets of Gorilla Dro Po Po, a substance they believed was synthetic cannabis. The district attorney refused to prosecute the case, however, because there was insufficient evidence that Gorilla Dro Po Po was illegal.

> Also at high risk for substance abuse are lesbian, gay, bisexual, and transgender (LGBT) teens.

When Gray went to Planet X, she identified herself as a reporter to the clerk behind the counter. She then asked the clerk if the store sold potpourri, which is a known code name for synthetic cannabis. The young man made it clear that they sold herbal incense, not potpourri. Gray then asked if the herbal incense could be smoked and the clerk replied no, that it was not for human consumption. When she requested that he show her a packet, he replied, "I would just rather not."[31]

In a later conversation with Planet X's attorney, David Martinez, Gray asked what product was the store selling, then, if not illegal substances? Martinez answered that the product was designed "to make a place smell good. Same stuff they sell at Wal-Mart."[32] Gray writes: "I tell him that based on the per-gram price, Planet X appears to be selling potpourri at something like $280 an ounce. (An ounce of potpourri at Wal-Mart costs about 40¢.) Martinez's response: 'There must be something in it that people like.'"[33]

Not Just for Pro Athletes

Because of widespread publicity, most people are well aware of famous athletes who have been caught using steroids and other performance-enhancing drugs (PEDs). What is less well known is that teens, most commonly boys, also use these drugs. "Many young people may feel pressured—by their peers or by their own ambitions—to use these drugs to improve their competitive performance, lose weight, or improve their own body image,"[34] says the patient education group SecondsCount, who reports that 5 percent of high school boys and 2 percent of high school girls use PEDs. One finding of the 2014 MTF survey is that steroid use, which peaked between 2000 and 2002, had markedly declined among teens in all three grades.

> As soon as certain compounds are added to state or federal lists of illegal substances, manufacturers simply tweak the formulas so they are no longer technically illegal.

The findings of another study, however, were not so good. In a 2013 survey of 3,705 high school students, the Partnership for Drug-Free Kids found that 11 percent had used synthetic human growth hormone (HGH) at least once—up from about 5 percent in the four preceding annual surveys. Also revealed was that, contrary to what was found in the MTF, teen use of steroids had increased from 5 percent to 7 percent over the period of time the five surveys were conducted. Former Olympic cyclist Tyler Hamilton, who in 2012 was found guilty of doping and stripped of his Olympic gold medal, explains the temptation to take PEDs: "There's so much pressure on winning—it's tough for these kids to stay true to themselves."[35]

High-Risk Teens

Although teens from all walks of life can (and do) become involved with alcohol and drugs, certain groups have a higher-than-average risk. One example is American Indian teens, who studies have shown are far more likely to use illicit drugs than non-Indian youth. One of these studies was published in September 2014. One of the most striking findings is a huge disparity in marijuana use. Between 2009 and 2012, 56.2 percent of American Indian eighth graders and 61.4 percent of tenth graders had used marijuana, compared with 16.4 percent of eighth graders and 33.4 percent of tenth graders in the general population. Over the same three-year period, yearly heroin and OxyContin use by American Indian teens was about two to three times higher than the national average. "This study is quite a wake-up call,"[36] says NIDA director Nora D. Volkow.

Also at high risk for substance abuse are lesbian, gay, bisexual, and transgender (LGBT) teens. Along with the stress that is common among all young people, LGBT teens must also deal with problems that are unique to them: their sexuality, feeling like they don't fit in, harassment by their peers and sometimes adults too—even their own families. It is not uncommon for LGBT youth to turn to alcohol or drugs in an attempt to escape from the pain associated with being different. Says psychologist Robin Barnett: "Substance abuse creates an emotional numbing agent, and also creates a deterrent from the real issue and the need to address it."[37]

Progress and Setbacks

Kids throughout the United States are drinking alcohol and taking drugs—that has been revealed in study after study. Through the years progress has been made in curbing alcohol use among teens, and use of some other drugs has slowed down as well. There is still a long way to go, however, because prevalence of alcohol and drug use is still high, and teen substance abuse remains a problem.

How Serious a Problem Is Substance Abuse Among Teens?

> 66 Teen prescription drug misuse and abuse continues to be a significant health problem threatening the well-being of American youth. 99

> —The Partnership for Drug-Free Kids and MetLife Foundation, "2012 Partnership Attitude Tracking Study," April 23, 2013. www.drugfree.org.

The Partnership for Drug-Free Kids is dedicated to helping parents and families solve the problem of teenage substance abuse, and the MetLife Foundation supports initiatives that focus on substance abuse prevention and education.

> 66 Misuse and abuse (or 'non-medical use') of prescription and over-the-counter drugs continues to decline among the nation's youth. 99

> —National Institute on Drug Abuse (NIDA), "High School and Youth Trends," *Drug Facts*, December 2014. www.drugabuse.gov.

An agency of the National Institutes of Health, the NIDA seeks to end drug abuse and addiction in the United States.

Bracketed quotes indicate conflicting positions.

* Editor's Note: While the definition of a primary source can be narrowly or broadly defined, for the purposes of Compact Research, a primary source consists of: 1) results of original research presented by an organization or researcher; 2) eyewitness accounts of events, personal experience, or work experience; 3) first-person editorials offering pundits' opinions; 4) government officials presenting political plans and/or policies; 5) representatives of organizations presenting testimony or policy.

❝The use of illegal drugs is increasing, especially among young teens. The average age of first marijuana use is 14, and alcohol use can start before age 12.❞

—American Academy of Child & Adolescent Psychiatry (AACAP), "Teens: Alcohol and Other Drugs," Facts for Families, July 2013. www.aacap.org.

The AACAP seeks to promote the healthy development of children, adolescents, and families through research, training, prevention, and treatment, while meeting the professional needs of child and adolescent psychiatrists.

❝Molly, a new version of an old drug, can be found spouted in hip-hop lyrics, passed around at music festivals, and experimented with in high schools and on college campuses. It's only growing in popularity and taking the nation's youth by storm.❞

—Anand Veeravagu, "Miley, Molly, and Your Teen's Mind," *Daily Beast*, May 13, 2014. www.thedailybeast.com.

Veeravagu is senior neurosurgery resident at Stanford University School of Medicine.

❝Regardless of what they have planned, one thing is for certain; alcohol will be a part of many teens' weekend plans and there's research to prove it.❞

—Raychelle Cassada Lohmann, "Teen Binge Drinking: All Too Common," *Psychology Today*, January 26, 2013. www.psychologytoday.com.

Lohmann is a family therapist from South Carolina and the author of several books for teens on coping with anger, angst, and bullying.

❝Teens are flocking to the Dark Net to purchase drugs and then having them delivered to their parents' mail box.❞

—Sedgrid Lewis, "Protect Your Teen from Dangerous Dark Net Drugs," *Huffington Post*, February 1, 2014. www.huffingtonpost.com.

Lewis is a cybercrime and Internet safety expert.

> **❝Alcohol use by persons under age 21 years is a major public health problem.❞**

—Centers for Disease Control and Prevention (CDC), "Fact Sheets—Underage Drinking," October 31, 2014. www.cdc.gov.

The CDC's mission is to protect the United States from health and safety threats, both foreign and domestic.

> **❝Most teens are smart enough to avoid anabolic steroids—synthetic hormones that add muscle and prevent muscle breakdown. But some student athletes may be tempted to use them.❞**

—Cleveland Clinic bone, muscle, and joint team, "Talking to Teens About Steroid Use," February 21, 2013. http://health.clevelandclinic.org.

The bone, muscle, and joint team at Cleveland Clinic in Cleveland, Ohio, is a group of medical professionals who diagnose, treat, and rehabilitate adults and children with disorders of the bone, joint, or connective tissue.

How Serious a Problem Is Substance Abuse Among Teens?

- An April 2013 Substance Abuse and Mental Health Services Administration report states that during 2010 and 2011 combined, **nearly 7 million teens** in the United States drank alcohol and **nearly 5 million** used an illicit drug.

- According to the Office of National Drug Control Policy, every day **4,000 young people aged 12 to 17** try drugs for the first time.

- In a 2013 survey of high school students by Mothers Against Drunk Driving (MADD), more than **three-fourths of teens** said they do not drink alcohol.

- In a 2012 survey by the National Center on Addiction and Substance Abuse at Columbia University (CASAColumbia), more than half of teens said that there is a place on or near school grounds where students go to use drugs, drink, and smoke during the school day.

- In a study published in July 2014 by Partnership for Drug-Free Kids and MetLife Foundation, **11 percent** of teens reported using synthetic human growth hormone (HGH) at least once within their lifetime, and **7 percent** of teens reported the same for steroids.

- The NIDA's 2014 Monitoring the Future survey found that **5.8 percent of high school seniors** in the United States used marijuana daily or nearly every day.

Most Commonly Abused Substances by Teens

During the 2014 Monitoring the Future survey, which involved more than 41,000 eighth, tenth, and twelfth graders throughout the United States, researchers asked teens what (if any) drugs they had used at least once during their lifetimes. As shown here, alcohol was by far the most common, followed by marijuana.

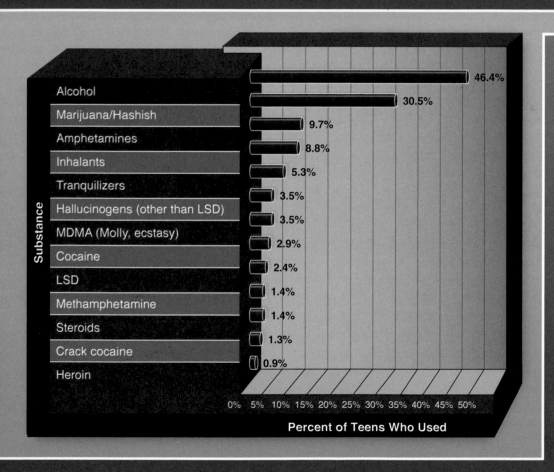

Lifetime prevalence of use of alcohol and various drugs for grades 8, 10, and 12 combined, 2014

Substance / Percent of Teens Who Used:

- Alcohol: 46.4%
- Marijuana/Hashish: 30.5%
- Amphetamines: 9.7%
- Inhalants: 8.8%
- Tranquilizers: 5.3%
- Hallucinogens (other than LSD): 3.5%
- MDMA (Molly, ecstasy): 3.5%
- Cocaine: 2.9%
- LSD: 2.4%
- Methamphetamine: 1.4%
- Steroids: 1.4%
- Crack cocaine: 1.3%
- Heroin: 0.9%

Source: Lloyd D. Johnston et al., "Monitoring the Future: 2014 Overview, Key Findings on Adolescent Drug Use," February 2015. www.monitoringthefuture.org.

Drinking Drops Among Teens; Drug Use Rises

The NIDA-sponsored Monitoring the Future survey, which is conducted each year with eighth, tenth, and twelfth graders throughout the United States, measures a number of behavioral factors, including substance use. One finding of the February 2014 survey was that drug use among young people has declined since 1991—but the same is not true of alcohol use. Although it has fluctuated widely over the years, teen alcohol use was found to be higher in 2014 than in 1991.

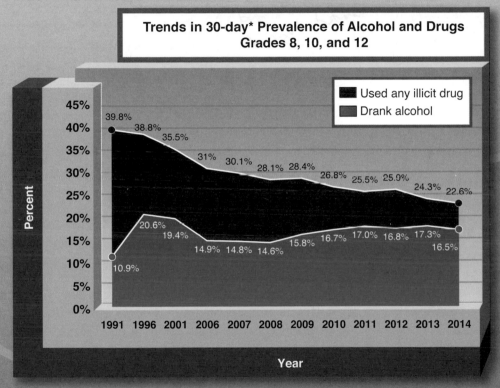

Trends in 30-day* Prevalence of Alcohol and Drugs Grades 8, 10, and 12

*30-day prevalence means having used alcohol and/or drugs at least one time in the past 30 days.

Source: Lloyd D. Johnston et al., "Monitoring the Future: 2014 Overview, Key Findings on Adolescent Drug Use," February 2015. www.monitoringthefuture.org.

- According to a March 2014 article by emergency medicine physician Robert Glatter, an estimated **2 out of 5 college students** take part in binge drinking.

Most Drug Use Starts During Adolescence

Although people of all ages are known to take drugs, national substance abuse surveys indicate that what NIDA calls the "drug danger zone" is between the ages of sixteen and seventeen, followed by eighteen- to twenty-year-olds.

The Drug Danger Zone:
Most Illicit Drug Use Starts in the Teenage Years

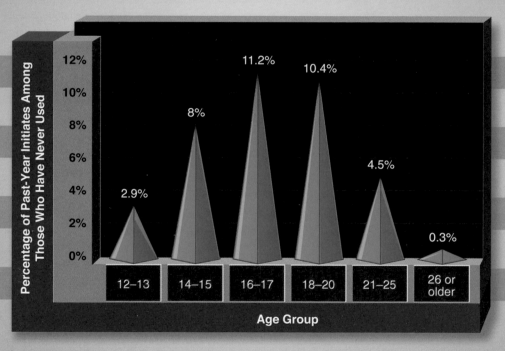

Source: National Institute on Drug Abuse, "Drugs, Brains, and Behavior: The Science of Addiction," July 2014. www.drugabuse.gov.

- The CDC's 2013 Youth Risk Behavior Surveillance, which was published in June 2014, found that the number of teens who were currently using alcohol had declined significantly, from **50.8 percent** in 1991 to **34.9 percent** in 2013.

Nearly One-Fourth of Twelfth Grade Males Are Binge Drinkers

Binge drinking is defined as having five or more alcoholic drinks in a row over a period of about two hours, and extreme binge drinking involves having ten to fifteen drinks in a row over the same period of time—an extremely dangerous practice. A study published in November 2013 found that both males and females had participated in binge drinking within two weeks prior to the study, but as shown here, males do so at a much higher rate.

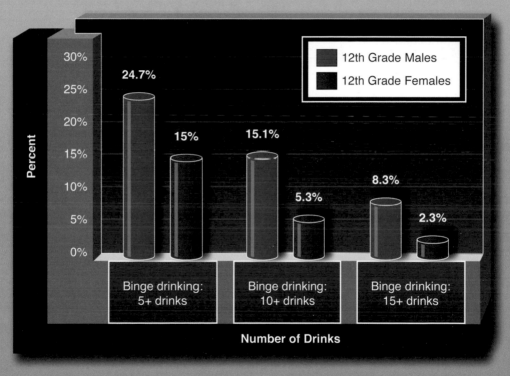

Source: Megan E. Patrick et al., "Extreme Binge Drinking Among 12th-Grade Students in the United States: Prevalence and Predictors," *JAMA Pediatrics*, November 2013. http://archpedi.jamanetwork.com.

- According to a 2014 paper by researchers Aaron White and Ralph Hingson, roughly **20 percent of college students** met the criteria for an alcohol use disorder in a given year (**8 percent** alcohol abuse, **13 percent** alcohol dependence).

Why Do Teens Use Alcohol and Drugs?

66Adolescents are 'biologically wired' to seek new experiences and take risks, as well as to carve out their own identity. Trying drugs may fulfill all of these normal developmental drives, but in an unhealthy way.99

—National Institute on Drug Abuse (NIDA), which seeks to end drug abuse and addiction in the United States.

66Drug use is typically an 'escape' for teens. It's important to seek help for the drug use, but more important, to find the cause of it.99

—Donna M. White, a licensed mental health counselor from South Carolina.

Although teenagers have many reasons for abusing substances, experts have identified some common traits. For instance, many teens drink alcohol, smoke pot, or use Molly because their friends are doing it and they do not want to feel left out. Maybe they are bored or restless and looking for something different to do. Or, they could be rebelling against their parents' authority while trying to assert their independence. One of the reasons teens cite most often when asked about substance abuse is peer pressure. The Promises Treatment Centers addiction program says that while peer pressure is a "powerful force at any stage of life," it is especially influential during adolescence. The group writes: "At a time when kids are trying to figure out who they are and where they fit in—when insecurities can be fierce—the desire to be accepted and liked makes saying 'no' extremely difficult. Saying no can also have painful consequences, ranging from being laughed at or mildly teased, to being humiliated, rejected, and even bullied."[38]

The Role of the Family

Psychologists have long known that family environment plays a major role in the choices a young person makes—including whether to use alcohol or drugs. That does not necessarily mean parents are to blame when teens get drunk or high; but what young people observe and are exposed to at home can definitely influence their decisions. "As children begin to grow and navigate the challenges of adolescence," says Elements Behavioral Health, "parental substance abuse has a direct impact on their well-being, as well as their behavior." The group adds that alcoholic parents often create an environment in which teens find it easy to drink. "This is largely because easy access to alcohol is readily available. In addition, a parent who is drunk may not know or even care that their teen is drinking."[39]

> " Many teens drink alcohol, smoke pot, or use Molly because their friends are doing it and they do not want to feel left out. "

A survey released in April 2014 by Mothers Against Drunk Driving (MADD) shows how much parents can influence teens' decisions about alcohol use. Nearly seven hundred high school students participated in the survey. Teens whose parents made it clear that underage drinking was unacceptable were 80 percent less likely to drink, compared with those whose parents were more lenient. Of the teens whose parents thought underage drinking was never acceptable, only 8 percent drank alcohol.

Coping with Stress

During the CASAColumbia substance abuse survey, which was published in August 2012, teens were asked to share their thoughts about why young people drink alcohol. The two main reasons cited were that

> **For most of the stressed-out teens, school was either a somewhat or significant reason for their stress.**

kids wanted to have fun, and were also influenced by peer pressure.

Another reason given by teens was stress, which studies have shown to be a major factor in the use of alcohol and drugs among young people. One of these studies was sponsored by the American Psychological Association (APA) in 2013. The researchers found that more than half of teens felt at least moderate stress during the school year, and 27 percent of those teens felt "extreme stress." For most of the stressed-out teens, school was either a somewhat or significant reason for their stress. This was also reflected during a study published in July 2014 by Partnership for Drug-Free Kids and MetLife Foundation. Teens who smoked marijuana were asked their reasons for doing so, and nearly one-third said it was to deal with school-related pressures and stress. Substance abuse professionals refer to this as self-medicating.

"Study Drugs"

When considering the issue of teen substance abuse, people typically think about alcohol, marijuana, MDMA, synthetic drugs, and other such commonly known substances. Many are unaware of another alarming trend: abuse of the prescription medications Adderall and Vyvanse. These drugs are prescribed for children and adolescents who are diagnosed with attention-deficit/hyperactivity disorder, better known as ADHD. Even though the drugs are amphetamines (members of the stimulant group), they have a surprisingly calming effect on those with ADHD.

Adderall and Vyvanse help ADHD sufferers stay focused and avoid distraction—a characteristic that has made the drugs appealing to many who do not have ADHD. A growing number of teens are taking Adderall or Vyvanse to stay awake late at night and maintain a laser-like focus throughout the school day. *New York Times* journalist Alan Schwarz writes:

> At high schools across the United States, pressure over grades and competition for college admissions are encouraging students to abuse prescription stimulants. . . .

Pills that have been a staple in some college and graduate school circles are going from rare to routine in many academically competitive high schools, where teenagers say they get them from friends, buy them from student dealers or fake symptoms to their parents and doctors to get prescriptions.[40]

Academic pressure during her senior year led to abuse of prescription drugs by a young woman named Madeleine. She attended a well-known private high school in Bethesda, Maryland, where she was taking five advanced placement classes. She was also a star player on the field hockey team and participated in other extracurricular activities as well. The pressure was starting to become unbearable, and Madeleine knew that something had to give, but she would not consider dropping any of her classes or activities. In an attempt to squeeze more hours out of each day, she started taking Adderall and Vyvanse.

> " Although ADHD drugs may be alluring to teens who have overloaded schedules, there are serious risks for anyone who uses the drugs for nonmedical purposes. "

Although ADHD drugs may be alluring to teens like Madeleine who have overloaded schedules, there are serious risks for anyone who uses the drugs for nonmedical purposes. Amphetamines are highly addictive, grouped by the DEA in the same category as cocaine and morphine. Prescription stimulants have been linked to depression and severe mood swings, often caused by lack of sleep. Especially frightening to health officials is the unknown, as Schwarz explains: "Little is known about the long-term effects of abuse of stimulants among the young. Drug counselors say that for some teenagers, the pills eventually become an entry to the abuse of painkillers and sleep aids."[41]

Shifting Perceptions of Risk

Studies have clearly shown a strong connection between what teens believe about alcohol and drugs (including their perceptions about harm) and whether they choose to use substances or turn away from them. In other words, young people who perceive alcohol and/or drugs to be harmful or who disapprove of people using them are much less likely to drink or do drugs themselves. The authors of the 2014 MTF survey emphasize that teen beliefs and attitudes are "particularly important in explaining trends in use."[42]

It is notable that, over time, teens' beliefs about substances being harmful and their disapproval of those who use the substances have diminished. This, experts say, has the potential to translate into increased use. For instance, in 1991 when high school sophomores were asked if they disapproved of people who smoked marijuana regularly, more than 90 percent answered yes, they did. When the same question was asked during the 2014 survey, the number who disapproved had dropped to 74.5 percent.

Even more profound was the changing attitude about possible harm. In 1991, when asked if they thought people risked harming themselves by smoking marijuana regularly, 82 percent of tenth graders said they believed it did—and by 2014 that number had dwindled to 45 percent. Among twelfth graders the decline in perceived risk was even more drastic. Close to 79 percent of seniors thought people who smoked pot were at great risk of harming themselves in 1991, and by 2014 the number had dropped by more than half. A particularly troubling finding was that only 24.3 percent of eighth graders thought it was risky to take MDMA once or twice. Even high school sophomores and seniors perceived a greater amount of risk than that. This is alarming to health officials because if teens do not think drugs are risky, they are much more likely to use them.

> " Adults often have trouble understanding why teens use alcohol or drugs. "

Teens may also be motivated to use drugs based on their perception that other young people are using them—yet research suggests that teens overestimate the extent to which other students use drugs. A study published in the December 2014 issue of *Developmental Psychology*, for example, found that teens believed certain groups of students binged on alcohol and smoked marijuana much more often than they actually did; furthermore, teens made decisions about whether to use substances based on these erroneous beliefs. As *Education Week* reporter Evie Blad explains: "Teens overestimate how often their peers participate in risky sexual and drug-related behaviors, and those misperceptions may cause them to adjust their own behaviors, adapting to social norms that don't actually exist."[43]

Brain Under Construction

Adults often have trouble understanding why teens use alcohol or drugs. This is true of many parents who feel frustrated when their teens make what seem to be obviously bad choices. Although there are many reasons why teens might make such choices, one is that adolescents' brains are not yet fully developed. "These brain differences don't mean that young people can't make good decisions or tell the difference between right and wrong," says the American Academy of Child & Adolescent Psychiatry. "It also doesn't mean that they shouldn't be held responsible for their actions. But an awareness of these differences can help parents, teachers, advocates, and policy makers understand, anticipate, and manage the behavior of adolescents."[44]

Years of research have been devoted to studying the human brain, with special attention given to the adolescent brain. Scientists have learned that the brain develops from back to front, and the last part to develop is the prefrontal cortex. This is located at the very front of the brain behind the forehead, and it controls such functions as reasoning, problem solving, impulse control, and decision making. Nora D. Volkow explains:

> The prefrontal cortex, where we make decisions and comparative judgments about the value of different courses of action, is crucial for regulating our behavior in the face of potential rewards like drugs and food. Adolescents are prone to risky behaviors and impulsive actions that provide instant gratification instead of eventual rewards. In part, this is because their prefrontal cortex is still a work in progress.[45]

Volkow goes on to say that the underdeveloped adolescent brain is a major factor in why young people are susceptible to taking drugs or drinking alcohol. "There are numerous pressures in their lives to try these substances (stress and peers, for example)," she says, "but inadequate cognitive resources to help them resist."[46]

Ongoing research to better understand brain development in young people is being conducted by neuroscientists as part of the Adolescent Development Study, which involves 135 preteen and teenage boys and girls ranging in age from eleven to thirteen. Researchers hope to identify brain factors and behaviors that put teens at risk of alcohol use and abuse even before they start drinking. "The primary goal of the Adolescent Development Study is to look at what's happening in the brains of adolescents before they have started drinking and doing drugs," says study codirector John VanMeter. "We know from lots of studies that if you look at teenagers who have started drinking and doing drugs that there are certain deficits in their brain, mainly in the prefrontal cortex. But the question is open as to whether some of these deficits predate the alcohol and drug use or are strictly a consequence."[47]

The young people participating in the study underwent several tests, including a brain scan known as an MRI, which allowed researchers to examine the connection between brain development and behavior. Thus far, VanMeter and his colleagues have discovered that teens at risk of future alcohol abuse have reduced connections in vital brain regions, greater impulsiveness, and lower levels of a fatty acid that is crucial for building brain tissue. As the study continues, the researchers hope to make additional discoveries about young brains that could lead to a better understanding of why teens choose to use drugs and alcohol.

Questions Linger

In an effort to better understand teen substance abuse and its causes, researchers employ a variety of methods such as surveys, brain studies, and other types of research. Although young people have their own personal reasons for getting involved with drugs and alcohol, typical influencers include peer pressure, stress, and naïveté about the risks involved, among other factors. The list of contributing factors will undoubtedly grow as research continues in the future.

Why Do Teens Use Alcohol and Drugs?

66 Genetic factors and life stressors influence adolescents' alcohol abuse. 99

—Office of Adolescent Health, "Alcohol," December 31, 2014. www.hhs.gov.

An agency of the US Department of Health and Human Services, the Office of Adolescent Health is dedicated to improving the health and well-being of adolescents to enable them to become healthy, productive adults.

66 Forget about blaming genetics as a reason for your problems with alcohol. Even if you do have a genetic marker that somehow increases your vulnerability, there are other factors that contribute to alcoholism besides genetics. 99

—Elements Behavioral Health, "Teens Stop Blaming Your Parents for Your Alcohol Problems," Addiction Intervention, 2015. www.addiction-intervention.com.

Elements Behavioral Health is a network of addiction treatment programs with facilities in Southern California; Nashville, Tennessee; and Fort Lauderdale, Florida.

* Editor's Note: While the definition of a primary source can be narrowly or broadly defined, for the purposes of Compact Research, a primary source consists of: 1) results of original research presented by an organization or researcher; 2) eyewitness accounts of events, personal experience, or work experience; 3) first-person editorials offering pundits' opinions; 4) government officials presenting political plans and/or policies; 5) representatives of organizations presenting testimony or policy.

"Teens often feel indestructible and might not consider the consequences of their actions, leading them to take dangerous risks—such as abusing legal or illegal drugs."

—Mayo Clinic, "Teen Drug Abuse: Help Your Teen Avoid Drugs," Tween and Teen Health, January 12, 2013. www.mayoclinic.org.

The Mayo Clinic is a world-renowned health care facility headquartered in Rochester, Minnesota.

"A teen living in a conflicted home environment may resort to drugs to shut out the world for a while—or at least make it feel a little more bearable."

—Promises Treatment Centers, "10 Reasons Teens Abuse Alcohol or Drugs," 2015. www.promises.com.

Promises Treatment Centers are addiction treatment facilities with two locations in Southern California and one in Austin, Texas.

"One reason kids may experiment with drugs is simply that they are bored."

—Drug Enforcement Administration (DEA), *Growing Up Drug Free*, October 2012. www.dea.gov.

The DEA is the United States' leading law enforcement agency for combating the sale and distribution of narcotics and other illegal drugs.

"Novelty-seeking, poor judgment, and risk-taking behavior are partly to blame for teenage binge drinking, but there is a social component as well."

—Frances E. Jensen, *The Teenage Brain*. New York: HarperCollins, 2015, p. 128.

Jensen is a neuroscientist from Philadelphia, Pennsylvania.

66 Moms and Dads who smoke cigarettes, abuse alcohol, smoke marijuana, and abuse prescription drugs are likelier to have kids who smoke cigarettes, abuse alcohol, smoke marijuana, and abuse prescription drugs. 99

—Joseph A. Califano Jr., *How to Raise a Drug-Free Kid*. New York: Touchstone, 2014, p. 19.

Califano is founder and former chairman of the National Center on Addiction and Substance Abuse at Columbia University.

66 There has been some indication that people who experiment with drugs and had been abused as children are more likely to develop a substance abuse disorder than their associates who had not suffered similar childhood abuse. 99

—Deborah A. Berberich, *Out of the Rabbit Hole: Breaking the Cycle of Addiction*. Bloomington, IN: Xlibris, 2013, p. 44.

Berberich is a clinical psychologist from Southern California who specializes in the treatment of addiction and mental illness.

66 Lack of parental supervision . . . can increase the likelihood that a child will abuse drugs, and a close parent-child bond can bolster a child's defenses against drug use. 99

—David Sack, "The Unlikely Force Driving Teen Prescription Drug Addiction: Parents?," *Huffington Post*, August 18, 2013. www.huffingtonpost.com.

Sack is a psychiatrist who serves as the CEO of a network of addiction treatment programs known as Elements Behavioral Health.

Why Do Teens Use Alcohol and Drugs?

- In a 2012 survey of high school juniors, seniors, and recent graduates, **62 percent of participants** said that seeing pictures of teenagers drinking on social media sites such as Facebook and Tumblr encourages other teens to want to drink.

- A study published in February 2015 by Idaho State University researchers found that inadequate sleep raised teenagers' risk of becoming involved with drugs and/or alcohol.

- According to the Promises treatment program, teens who struggle with emotional pain are especially vulnerable to alcohol and drug abuse.

- In a study published in July 2014 by Partnership for Drug-Free Kids and MetLife Foundation, **15 percent of teens** who abused prescription drugs did so in an effort to relax.

- Ready access has been shown to be a strong contributor to teen substance abuse; for example, according to the antidrug group DoSomething.org, **60 percent of teens** who abuse prescription drugs get them free from friends and relatives.

- A September 2013 fact sheet by the Child Trends DataBank cites a study showing that adolescents who did not plan to complete four years of college were much more likely to abuse alcohol or drugs than their peers who did plan to attend college for four years.

Teens Prescribed Certain Drugs Most Likely to Abuse Them Later

Research has shown that most teens who abuse prescription drugs (using them for nonmedical purposes) get the drugs from someone they know, such as friends or family members. To determine whether teens who were once legitimately prescribed anti-anxiety or sleep medications found a way to continue taking them after their prescription expired, University of Michigan researchers conducted a three-year survey of 2,745 teens. As shown here, the teens who had previously taken the drugs by prescription were more likely to become dependent and abuse the drugs later.

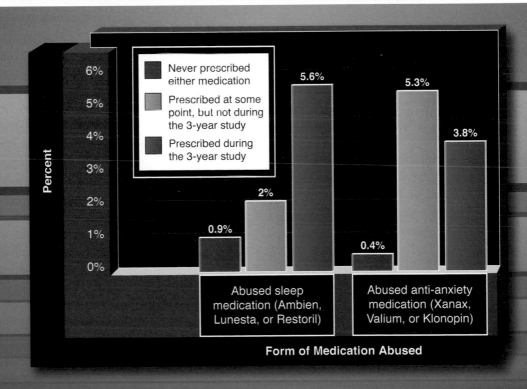

Source: Carol J. Boyd et al., "A Prospective Study of Adolescents' Nonmedical Use of Anxiolytic and Sleep Medication," Psychology of Addictive Behavior, November 2014. www.apa.org.

What Teens Say About Their Use of Marijuana

In a 2013 survey by Partnership for Drug-Free Kids and MetLife Foundation, teens who said they used marijuana were asked to share their reasons for doing so. As shown here, the main reason was to have fun, followed by relaxation.

Question: What was the main reason you last used marijuana?

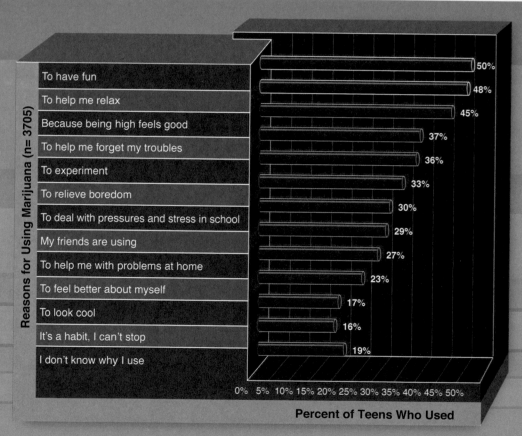

Reasons for Using Marijuana (n= 3705)

Reason	Percent
To have fun	50%
To help me relax	48%
Because being high feels good	45%
To help me forget my troubles	37%
To experiment	36%
To relieve boredom	33%
To deal with pressures and stress in school	30%
My friends are using	29%
To help me with problems at home	27%
To feel better about myself	23%
To look cool	17%
It's a habit, I can't stop	16%
I don't know why I use	19%

0% 5% 10% 15% 20% 25% 30% 35% 40% 45% 50%

Percent of Teens Who Used

Source: Partnership for Drug-Free Kids and MetLife Foundation, "The Partnership Attitude Tracking Study: Teens & Parents 2013," July 2014. www.drugfree.org.

- The Mayo Clinic states that some teens use performance-enhancing drugs as a way to cope with body image insecurities or to fit in with a group of peers.

- A 2015 study led by Susanne Tanski of the Geisel School of Medicine at Dartmouth College found a link between the number of television ads for alcohol that teens are exposed to and their odds for problem drinking.

- According to Emily Feinstein, CASAColumbia's director of health law and policy, research shows that teens who drink alcohol with their parents at home are more likely to drink outside of the home and without parental supervision.

- According to CRC Health Group in Cupertino, California, teens who struggle with mental health issues or behavioral disorders, especially those that remain undiagnosed, may turn to substance abuse as a misguided attempt to self-medicate.

- In a study published in July 2014 by Partnership for Drug-Free Kids and MetLife Foundation, **37 percent of teens** who smoked marijuana said they did it to help forget their troubles.

- According to the Mayo Clinic, teens with an immediate family member (such as a parent or sibling) with alcohol or drug problems have a higher-than-normal risk of developing a drug addiction.

What Are the Consequences of Substance Abuse?

66 The person you shape while growing up can be the person you're stuck with. So allowing drugs or alcohol to influence this young person can affect not just who you are today, but who you can be and will become. 99

—Richard Taite, founder and CEO of the addiction treatment facility Cliffside Malibu Rehab Center and coauthor of the book *Ending Addiction for Good*.

66 Some teens will experiment and stop, or continue to use occasionally, without significant problems. Others will develop a dependency, moving on to more dangerous drugs and causing significant harm to themselves and possibly others. 99

—American Academy of Child & Adolescent Psychiatry, which is committed to the physical, mental, and social health and well-being of all infants, children, adolescents, and young adults.

D akota Dyer was one of those teens who seemed to have everything going for him. The fourteen-year-old from Bremen, Georgia, loved animals and being outdoors and had been the recipient of a prestigious community service award for an environmental project in which he cleaned up a polluted creek and reintroduced frogs and salamanders into the water. He also loved football and played starting defensive end on his middle school team. He was an above-average student, had tons of friends, and was known for being kind; according to Lance Dyer, his son "had a knack for always being the one who took up for anyone who was being picked on."[48] One thing that did not interest Dakota was drugs— until March 2012 when he smoked a type of synthetic cannabis called "Mr. Miyagi Timeout." Its effects were immediate and drastic, causing him to snap, experiencing what was later called a psychotic break—a complete loss of touch with reality. For no apparent reason, and without any warning, Dakota found a handgun in his family home, put the gun to his head, and fired it, killing himself with a single shot. "His mother and I can only imagine the war he was fighting inside himself," says Lance Dyer, "due to the effects of this synthetic drug that would cause him to seek such a permanent, devastating solution."[48]

Emily's Story

Dakota's death was one of many catastrophes that have befallen young people who have experimented with synthetic cannabis, which experts say is an extremely dangerous, toxic drug. Like Dakota, Emily Bauer had a psychotic break after smoking it. She did not take her own life and in fact survived the episode. But the drug caused such severe damage to her body that doctors did not expect her to live.

The horrifying incident occurred in 2012, when Bauer was a sophomore in high school. She had purchased Spice at a local gas station and had been smoking it for a week or two. On December 7 of that year, within minutes of taking a few hits of Spice, Bauer developed a migraine headache and went to lie down for a nap. When she woke up, it seemed to her family that a completely different person had taken her place. She was stumbling around the house, slurring her words when she tried to speak, screaming, and acting violently. Her family called 911, and paramedics arrived, strapped her to a gurney, and rushed her to the hospital, where she screamed and flailed

> " For no apparent reason, and without any warning, Dakota found a handgun in his family home, put the gun to his head, and fired it, killing himself with a single shot. "

> "Synthetic cannabis has been tied to many deaths as well as hundreds of visits to emergency departments throughout the country and is extremely unpredictable."

and tried to bite medical personnel who were trying to help her.

Twenty-four hours later Bauer was no better. She was still exhibiting psychotic, violent behavior, so doctors put her into a medically induced coma. Tests showed bleeding on the brain and severe brain damage from several strokes. When doctors said there was no hope for Bauer to ever recover, her devastated family decided to take her off life support a few days before her seventeenth birthday—yet the doctors were wrong. Bauer woke up, smiled at her mother, and whispered that she loved her. She has fought hard to recover since that time and has made slow but steady progress. In September 2013 Bauer returned to her high school in Cypress, Texas. She has permanent brain damage, is still partially blind, and can no longer read or write, but her family is grateful that they still have her in their lives.

Dangerous and Unpredictable

Although the experiences of Emily Bauer and Dakota Dyer are extreme, they offer a glimpse at how dangerous synthetic drugs can be. Synthetic cannabis has been tied to many deaths as well as hundreds of visits to emergency departments throughout the country and is extremely unpredictable; even the scientist who created it says so. Organic chemist John W. Huffman developed about five hundred synthetic compounds (many of which were cannabinoids) that were created solely for research purposes, including pain management studies. The chemicals were never meant for use by humans, yet Huffman had no way to stop unscrupulous chemists from plucking his formulas out of scientific journals and using them to make and sell synthetic versions of marijuana—which they deceptively claimed were safe as well as legal. "I figured that somewhere along the line, some enterprising individual would try to smoke it,"[49] he says.

But even if Huffman cannot control the creation and distribution of synthetic cannabis, he can—and does—speak out against its use, warning people to stay away from it. He is quite candid and does not mince words, using terms like "incredibly foolish" and "idiotic" in reference to anyone who uses the drug. "I mean, it's just like taking a pistol with one bullet in it and spinning the chamber and holding it to your head and pulling the trigger,"[50] he says.

The synthetic drugs known as bath salts were also never intended for human use. When medicinal chemist Richard A. Glennon created synthetic cathinones, he was experimenting with stimulants and hallucinogens to evaluate how they affected the brain. But as with Huffman, Glennon's formulas were used by rogue chemists to make drugs that are as dangerous as synthetic cannabis and in some ways even more so. Medical professionals who have encountered people high on bath salts describe their behavior as bizarre and frightening. According to Mark Ryan, who directs the Louisiana Poison Control Center, the patients are psychotic and extremely difficult to handle. "For lack of a better term, they're flipped out,"[51] he says.

An especially disturbing characteristic of bath salts is that its effects linger in the body for a very long time; people have been known to still be paranoid days or even weeks after they use the drugs. Scientists attribute this lasting quality to the powerful stimulant methylenedioxypyrovalerone (MDPV), which is the main psychoactive component in synthetic cathinones and is up to ten times stronger than cocaine. Although research on these chemicals is still new, scientists have discovered that once MDPV latches onto brain cells, it sticks to them like glue. "MDPV is irreversible, it won't let go," says Virginia Commonwealth University researcher Louis J. De Felice. "I don't know of any other drug that has that same feature of not allowing you to escape from it."[52]

When Alcohol Is a Poison

Alcohol is deeply ingrained in many aspects of society; young people see their parents drink at home and in restaurants. They hear about drinking episodes in their favorite songs and see accounts on Facebook, Tumblr, and Twitter of other teens or celebrities doing shots and partying. Because of all the exposure and the way alcohol is glamorized in the media, teens are often not aware of how damaging it can be to their brains— much more so than to the brains of adults. "A young person's body cannot cope with alcohol the same way an adult's can," says the Foundation for a Drug-Free World. "Drinking is more harmful to teens than adults because their brains are still developing throughout adolescence and well into young adulthood. Drinking during this critical growth period can lead to lifelong damage in brain function, particularly as it relates to memory, motor skills (ability to move) and coordination."[53]

One of the greatest risks to teens when they drink heavily is alcohol poisoning. This is the potentially deadly result of drinking excessive amounts of alcohol in a short period of time. "It is caused by alcohol slowing down the body's functions (for example, breathing, heart rate, and gag reflex)," says physician Roxanne Dryden-Edwards, "thereby potentially leading to choking, coma, stopped breathing, stopped heart, and death. Treatment involves getting the person to the hospital immediately so he or she can be closely watched by medical professionals, given oxygen and fluids, and so that other measures can be taken in order to prevent choking, as well as stopped breathing or heartbeat."[54]

> " Because of all the exposure and the way alcohol is glamorized in the media, teens are often not aware of how damaging it can be to their brains—much more so than to the brains of adults. "

Sixteen-year-old Tori Adams came perilously close to dying from alcohol poisoning in May 2013. She had been staying with a friend's family at a beach house in Palm Island, Florida, and people were doing a lot of drinking. Adams did not usually drink, but that night she decided to join in with the partying. "I was taking multiple shots," she says. "I was drinking Captain Morgan in the beginning and then someone brought out 151 alcohol [rum with extremely high alcohol content], and I didn't know my limits. I took a shot of that and I sat down on the couch. That's when everything went black."[55]

Seeing that Adams had passed out, her friend acted quickly by calling 911—and saving her life in the process. She was airlifted via helicopter to a hospital where she underwent emergency treatment for alcohol poisoning. When she opened her eyes and saw that she was in a hospital room with IVs in her arms and a tube up her nose, she began to panic because she had no memory of what happened or how she got there. The doctor explained that she had nearly died. "He told me that if it weren't for my friend's judgment for calling for help instead of putting [me] to bed to sleep it off," says Adams, "I would not have survived."[56]

The Dark Side of Pot

Over the years society has become much more accepting of marijuana for medicinal as well as recreational use. Yet no matter what people may think about adults using the drug, studies have shown there are serious risks for teens who smoke marijuana on a regular basis. Experts warn that teens who smoke pot can suffer from a lack of motivation, destroyed creativity, personality changes, and reduced resistance to disease. Severe paranoia has also been linked to marijuana use among teens. A young man named Paul lived through this kind of nightmare, as he writes: "I became so paranoid that I successfully drove everyone away and found myself in the terrible place no one wants to be in—I was alone. I'd wake up in the morning and start using and keep using throughout the day."[57]

According to the American College of Pediatricians (ACPeds), health risks associated with marijuana are often grossly underestimated not only by teenagers, but also health care professionals and parents. "Parents underestimate the availability of marijuana to teens, the extent of their use of the drug, and the risks associated with its use,"[58] the group explains. The ACPeds cites a major National Academy of Sciences study published in 2012 that revealed objective evidence of marijuana being harmful to the brains of adolescents. A team of researchers in New Zealand administered IQ tests to more than one thousand thirteen-year-olds. Over the following years, as the teens aged, the researchers assessed their patterns of marijuana use at several points. Participants underwent IQ testing again at age thirty-eight, and the two scores were compared. "The results were striking," says the ACPeds. The group continues:

> " According to the American College of Pediatricians, health risks associated with marijuana are often grossly underestimated. "

Participants who used cannabis heavily in their teens and continued through adulthood showed a significant drop in IQ between the ages of 13 and 38—an average of eight points for those who met criteria for cannabis dependence. Those who started using marijuana regularly or heavily after age 18 showed minor declines. By comparison, those who never used marijuana showed no declines in IQ. . . . This means the finding of a significant mental decline among those who used marijuana heavily before age 18, even after they quit taking the drug, is consistent with the theory that drug use during adolescence—when the brain is still rewiring, pruning, and organizing itself—has long-lasting negative effects on the brain.[59]

Dangers Lurk

The consequences of teens drinking and using drugs are many, varied, and frightening. Synthetic cannabis and cathinones were never intended for human use, yet they are used by humans, and their effects are unpredictable and potentially lethal. Alcohol may be viewed by teens as a way to have fun with their friends, but in large doses it can be a deadly poison. Marijuana may be more acceptable to society in general, but when used habitually by teens it could potentially cause permanent damage to the brain. Teens who give careful consideration to these and other risks may decide that such substances are not for them after all.

What Are the Consequences
of Substance Abuse?

66 Impaired memory or thinking ability and other problems caused by drug use can derail a young person's
social and educational development and hold him or
her back in life. 99

> —National Institute on Drug Abuse (NIDA), "Principles of Adolescent Substance Use Disorder Treatment: A Research-
> Based Guide," January 17, 2014. www.drugabuse.gov.

An agency of the National Institutes of Health, the NIDA seeks to end drug abuse
and addiction in the United States.

....

66 Young people who occasionally smoke marijuana may
be rewiring their brains, with their pot use causing
structural changes to brain regions related to motivation, emotion and reward. 99

> —Ray Sahelian, "Marijuana Smoking Safety, Danger, Medicinal Uses, Health Risks and Benefits," November 16, 2014.
> www.raysahelian.com.

Sahelian is a physician from Southern California who specializes in wellness and
nutrition.

....

* Editor's Note: While the definition of a primary source can be narrowly or broadly defined, for the purposes of Compact
Research, a primary source consists of: 1) results of original research presented by an organization or researcher; 2) eyewitness
accounts of events, personal experience, or work experience; 3) first-person editorials offering pundits' opinions; 4) government
officials presenting political plans and/or policies; 5) representatives of organizations presenting testimony or policy.

Primary Source Quotes

66 So, what's the big deal of downing 4 or 5 drinks, right? Wrong! Binge drinking is actually extremely dangerous.**99**

—Raychelle Cassada Lohmann, "Teen Binge Drinking: All Too Common," *Psychology Today*, January 26, 2013. www.psychologytoday.com.

Lohmann is a family therapist from South Carolina and the author of several books for teens on coping with anger, angst, and bullying.

66 Although alcohol can be more damaging over a longer period of time, methamphetamine and other synthetic drugs such as ecstasy can do more extensive neurological damage in a far shorter period of time.**99**

—Deborah A. Berberich, *Out of the Rabbit Hole: Breaking the Cycle of Addiction*. Bloomington, IN: Xlibris, 2013, p. 36.

Berberich is a clinical psychologist from Southern California who specializes in the treatment of addiction and mental illness.

66 The most commonly abused prescription drugs, such as Xanax, OxyContin and Vicodin, now cause more deaths than heroin and cocaine combined.**99**

—David Sack, "The Unlikely Force Driving Teen Prescription Drug Addiction: Parents?," *Huffington Post*, August 18, 2013. www.huffingtonpost.com.

Sack is a psychiatrist who specializes in addiction.

66 The scientific evidence is now overwhelming that teen alcohol and drug abuse interferes with brain development and can inflict serious, sometimes irreversible, brain damage in the long term.**99**

—Joseph A. Califano Jr., *How to Raise a Drug-Free Kid*. New York: Touchstone, 2014, p. 14.

Califano is founder and former chairman of the National Center on Addiction and Substance Abuse at Columbia University.

66 Health risks associated with marijuana use are often underestimated by adolescents, their parents, and health professionals. 99

—American College of Pediatricians, "Marijuana Use: Detrimental to Youth," October 2014. www.acpeds.org.

The American College of Pediatricians is an organization of pediatricians and other health care professionals who are dedicated to the health and well-being of children.

66 The abuse of anabolic steroids can cause both temporary and permanent injury to anyone using them. Teenagers, whose bodies are still developing, are at heightened risk. 99

—US Food and Drug Administration (FDA), "Teens and Steroids: A Dangerous Combo," FDA Consumer Health Information, November 2013. www.fda.gov.

The FDA is a consumer protection agency that ensures the safety and efficacy of food, drugs, and veterinary products.

66 Drinking endangers adolescents in multiple ways including motor vehicle crashes, the leading cause of death for this age group. 99

—Office of Adolescent Health, "Substance Abuse," January 2, 2015. www.hhs.gov.

An agency of the US Department of Health and Human Services, the Office of Adolescent Health is dedicated to improving the health and well-being of adolescents to enable them to become healthy, productive adults.

Facts and Illustrations

What Are the Consequences of Substance Abuse?

- According to the National Council on Alcoholism and Drug Dependence, young people who start drinking alcohol before **age 15** are **five times** more likely to abuse alcohol or become dependent on it than those who first used alcohol at **age 21 or older**.

- In a 2014 study published by Partnership for Drug-Free Kids and MetLife Foundation, **85 percent of teens** said they recognize the risks involved with misusing and abusing prescription drugs.

- According to the Mayo Clinic, methamphetamine, opiates, and cocaine are highly addictive and cause multiple short-term and long-term health consequences, including psychotic behavior, seizures, or death due to overdose.

- The antidrug group DoSomething.org states that more teens die from prescription drugs than from heroin and cocaine combined.

- The Substance Abuse and Mental Health Services Administration reports that emergency room visits involving MDMA grew **128 percent** between 2005 and 2011 in **patients younger than 21**.

- According to the National Council on Alcoholism and Drug Dependence, an estimated **1,900 young people under age 21** die each year from alcohol-related motor vehicle crashes.

Facts and Illustrations

58

Teens Reveal Problems from Drinking, Pot Smoking

Experts cite numerous risks for teens who use alcohol and drugs, from damaged relationships to serious health issues. As part of a 2014 study by researchers from New York University, high school seniors who said they had drunk alcohol and/or used marijuana were asked about negative effects they had experienced. These graphs show the most common negative effects experienced by teens who had drunk alcohol or used marijuana more than ten times during their lives.

Top Five Adverse Effects of Alcohol Use

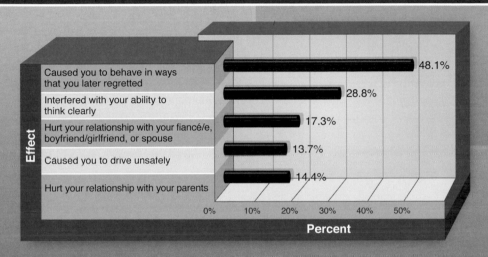

Top Five Adverse Effects of Marijuana

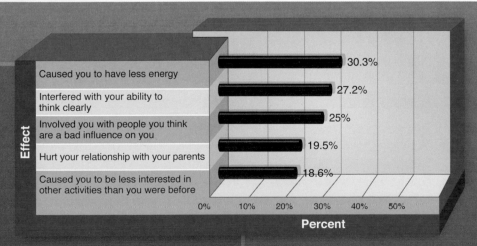

Source: Joseph J. Palamar et al., "Adverse Psychosocial Outcomes Associated with Drug Use Among US High School Seniors: A Comparison of Alcohol and Marijuana," *American Journal of Drug and Alcohol Abuse*, September 2014. http://informahealthcare.com.

Not Worth the Risk

Substance abuse experts say that every time teens drink alcohol or use drugs, they are risking their health and well-being. Shown here are some of the primary risks involved.

Risk	Result
Problems at school	Inability to concentrate and study, academic failure, leading to trouble getting into college and inability to find a good job as an adult.
Trouble with parents and teachers	Changes in personality: teens often become withdrawn, depressed, and angry more easily, resulting in strained relationships with parents and teachers.
Trouble with the law	Drugs cause teens to make poor decisions leading to drunk/drugged driving, fights, and unsafe sex. Also, teens may steal to support their habit, or become involved with vandalism or violent acts because of the people they spend time with.
Physical and mental health problems	Substance abuse can damage the brain, leading to seizures, memory loss, and other, more severe complications. Drug use can lead to health problems such as liver and kidney failure and irregular heart rate. With many drugs teens risk overdose and death even if they only use a drug once.
Drug addiction and alcoholism	Studies have shown that up to 90 percent of people who are addicted began using drugs and/or alcohol while they were in high school.

Source: MFI Recovery Center, "5 Reasons Why Teens Should Not Drink and Do Drugs," August 27, 2013. www.mfirecovery.com.

- In a March 2014 article, emergency medicine physician Robert Glatter cites a study that revealed students who binge drink once or twice during a two-week period are **nearly three times** as likely as non–binge drinkers to experience a blackout, suffer an injury, have a run-in with the police, or drive after consuming alcohol.

Molly Landing More Teens in the ER

The drug MDMA, which is often called Molly, has been shown to be unpredictable as well as dangerous for those who have taken it. One indication that Molly-related health issues are growing is the rising number of visits to emergency rooms throughout the country. Although ER visits involving MDMA in young people declined between 2010 and 2011, they are significantly higher than in 2005.

Emergency Room Visits Involving MDMA in Patients Younger than 21

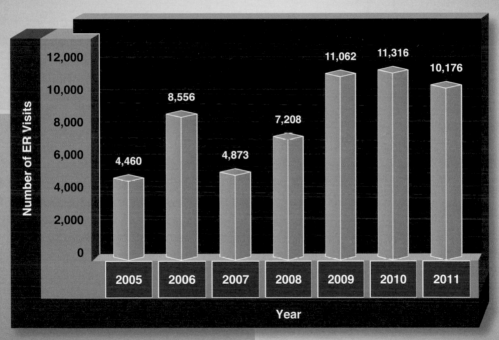

Source: Substance Abuse and Mental Health Services Administration, "Ecstasy-Related Emergency Department Visits by Young People Increased Between 2005 and 2011; Alcohol Involvement Remains a Concern," *The DAWN Report*, December 3, 2013. www.samhsa.gov.

- According to NIDA director Nora D. Volkow, teens who ingest or snort the synthetic drug known as bath salts can develop increased blood pressure, rapid heart rate, agitation, hallucinations, extreme paranoia, and delusions.

What Can Be Done About Teen Substance Abuse?

> **❝'Just say no'? It's a start, but few teens bent on enticing a peer to try drugs will let the matter rest there.❞**
>
> —American Academy of Pediatrics, which is committed to the physical, mental, and social health and well-being of all infants, children, adolescents, and young adults.

> **❝When research-based substance use prevention programs are properly implemented by schools and communities, use of alcohol, tobacco, and illegal drugs is reduced.❞**
>
> —National Institute on Drug Abuse (NIDA), which seeks to end drug abuse and addiction in the United States.

In February 2015, at an early morning assembly, a high school auditorium in Downingtown, Pennsylvania, was packed with several hundred teens—and what they saw and heard left them shaken. The students were watching a presentation by the drug education group Narcotics Overdose Prevention and Education (NOPE). One of the most jarring parts of the program was a recording of a 911 call by a frantic, terrified mother who had just found her teenage son dead of a prescription painkiller overdose. As the recording played the students were shown photo after photo of young people who had died from using drugs. They also looked at the teen who had overdosed; or rather, at the urn that contained his ashes. "All these kids were around our age," says Michael Senn, a high school senior who attended the presentation. "It felt personal."[60]

A Brutally Honest Approach

The NOPE program was created in 2002 in Palm Beach County, Florida, by community leaders, parents who had lost children to drug-related incidents, and others who were interested in helping. The organization's mission is to raise awareness among young people of the multitude of risks associated with drug and alcohol abuse. Students in middle schools and high schools watch dramatic multimedia presentations that are purposely blunt, often shocking, and intended to evoke powerful emotions. As high school students entered an auditorium for a January 30, 2014, presentation in Delaware County, Delaware, they were chatting with each other and laughing. Then the program started and there was complete silence. Except for soft crying sounds from some of the students, the auditorium remained silent during the entire presentation.

One of the presenters was Tricia Stouch, who spoke about how her nineteen-year-old daughter, Pamela, had died after a long, painful battle with drug abuse. "It's too late for my daughter," Stouch said. "But I might be able to help somebody else's child."[61] Accompanied by her oldest daughter, Colleen, Stouch stood at the podium and talked about how Pamela had gotten into a downward spiral from which she could not escape, and also spoke frankly of how Pamela's drug problem and death devastated her family. Colleen read from her sister's diary entry titled, "Why I use," which was Pamela's chronicle of her drug addiction and her fear that she would never be able to escape from it—a fear that proved to be true.

> **Except for soft crying sounds from some of the students, the auditorium remained silent during the entire presentation.**

NOPE training manager Laura Guelzow also played a role in the Delaware County presentation. With an array of huge photographs of teens who died of prescription drug or heroin overdose looming in the background, Guelzow discussed how the abuse of prescription drugs and heroin was affecting communities throughout the United States. Pointing to each of the pictures behind her she told the tragic story of each teen, including the youngest who was only thirteen years old. Another photo showed an eighteen-year-old boy dressed in a tuxedo, and beneath that was a picture of him lying dead in a casket. "All of the kids pictured here could have been saved," Guelzow told the group. "Others knew they were doing drugs and were afraid to tell." Guelzow explained that one of NOPE's primary goals is to empower students to become "heroes" to their friends and family members by speaking up about their friends' drug problems rather than remaining silent. "We need the students to realize it's not telling or snitching and that these are life and death situations," she says. "Every story behind me had missed opportunities."[62]

Above the Influence

Another antidrug program is Above the Influence (ATI), which was launched in November 2005 by the antidrug group Partnership for a Drug-Free America (now known as Partnership for Drug-Free Kids). This program aims to give teenagers the information they need to make smart, healthy decisions about alcohol and drugs. A November 2013 article in *Addiction Treatment Magazine* explains: "Above the Influence goes beyond simply preaching to kids that abusing alcohol or drugs is bad or telling them 'Don't do it.' Rather, its goal is to get tweens and teens to value their autonomy and independence so they won't choose to self-destruct through substance abuse."[63]

ATI connects with young people in a number of different ways, such as through its website, Facebook, Twitter, and also YouTube, where teens can choose from numerous ATI videos that are encouraging and inspiring. The ATI Facebook page (which has nearly 2 million followers) features posts and video clips about topics such as self-confidence and self-worth. Yet teens are not limited in what they want to discuss; they are invited to share their thoughts about everything from fashion and celebrities to sports. "For adults, it might not seem like those topics play into drug and alcohol abuse prevention," says the Partnership for Drug-Free Kids. "However, having conversations with youth about subjects that interest them shows the kids their opinions have value."[64]

On the social network site Tumblr, which features the popular micro-blogging format, teens can interact with each other about all kinds of topics, including current alcohol- and drug-related issues. When they click onto ATI's site on Tumblr, they see a message that is designed to inspire, motivate, and empower: "Every day, you face pressure to be different things for different people—fit in, stand out, fall in line, test the rules. No wonder it's easy to lose track of who you really are. But you have another option. Press pause, hit reset, and remember that it's up to you. You are Above the Influence."[65] Teens use the ATI Tumblr site to have conversations about topics that interest them or that they find troubling. For example, in July 2013, when *Glee* actor Cory Monteith died from an overdose of heroin mixed with alcohol, ATI invited teens to join a conversation about drug and alcohol addiction.

> "On the social network site Tumblr, which features the popular micro-blogging format, teens can interact with each other about all kinds of topics, including current alcohol- and drug-related issues."

One city where ATI programs have been successful is Saginaw, Alabama. Since 2006 the programs have been in place at Riverchase Middle School and Pelham High School in Saginaw. Volunteer Windy Rosenstiel was instrumental in bringing the programs to the schools after suffering personal tragedy. Her father battled drug abuse and finally died because of drugs, and she also witnessed other family members struggle with addiction. By sharing her story with young people, Rosenstiel hopes to broaden their knowledge about the risks involved with substance abuse. That, she hopes, will influence them to avoid using alcohol and drugs. "This program does not leave the user out," says Rosenstiel. "I tell them 'If you're going to put something in your body, at least educate yourself about what it is you're putting in your body.'"[66]

Parents Matter

Young people can be headstrong during the teenage years, often going out of their way to assert their independence and make their own decisions. Sometimes parents feel like their kids do not even like them, let alone care what they think. Yet as challenging as those years can be, psychologists say that teens still want—and need—parental supervision and guidance, especially when it comes to substance abuse.

Experts widely agree that good parenting is a crucial component of any effort to prevent young people from becoming involved with alcohol or drugs. "Parents have more influence over their child than friends, music, TV, the Internet and celebrities,"[67] says the Partnership for Drug-Free Kids. Yet research has shown that parents often underestimate how much influence they have over their children. In a Substance Abuse and Mental Health Services Administration (SAMHSA) study published in May 2013, more than one out of five parents of teens believed they had little influence on whether their child used alcohol, drugs, or tobacco products. The survey also found that nearly one in ten parents had not even attempted to talk about substance abuse with their teens.

Research has shown that teens from families in which underage drinking and using drugs are considered unacceptable are much less likely to develop substance abuse problems. "Parental expectations, particularly expressing strong disapproval of substance abuse, can be a decisive factor in their teens' behavior," says CASAColumbia founder Joseph A. Califano. "Teens who say their parents would be extremely upset to find out their child smokes, drinks or uses marijuana are less likely to use these substances or to say that it's okay for teens their age to smoke, get drunk and use marijuana."[68]

> " Sometimes parents feel like their kids do not even like them, let alone care what they think. "

According to Califano, there is a stark difference in attitude between teens who know their parents disapprove of alcohol and drug use and those who say their parents would not disapprove. Teens in the latter group are eight and one-half times likelier to say it is okay for kids their age to smoke marijuana. In addition, those teens are ten times more likely to think it is okay for other teens to get drunk. Says Califano: "We believe that, armed with information about the world their teens are living in, parents can be a powerful, and indeed decisive, influence on the behavior of their children."[69]

When talking with young people about substance abuse, parents should discuss the risks involved with using drugs and alcohol and clearly explain the rules regarding the use of these substances. This should be combined with an open, caring relationship, as a September 2013 publication by the research group Child Trends explains: "Adolescents who feel that they can trust and communicate with their parents are more likely to follow family rules."[70]

Teens Helping Teens

Surveys have shown that some of the most effective anti–substance-abuse programs are those in which young people help each other. One that has proved to help many teens is Teen Addiction Anonymous, better known as Teen AA. Designed by teens for teens, Teen AA helps young people kick drug and alcohol addiction and also rid themselves of destructive behaviors.

In 2012 health officials in Arizona decided to try Teen AA after receiving some very disturbing news. In the CDC's Youth Risk Behavior Surveillance, which evaluates teen alcohol and drug use (among other behaviors), Arizona ranked among the worst. Of all the states, Arizona had the highest rate of high school students who were offered, sold, or given an illegal drug by someone on school property, as well as the highest rate of binge drinking. Arizona teens ranked second out of all other states in five categories: those who had ever used cocaine, and who currently used cocaine; those who tried marijuana for the first time before age thirteen; those who were currently drinking alcohol; and those who had consumed alcohol on school property.

> **Research has shown that teens from families in which underage drinking and using drugs are considered unacceptable are much less likely to develop substance abuse problems.**

Determined to turn this situation around, Arizona health officials implemented Teen AA programs at high schools throughout the state, including about twenty in the Phoenix area. One of the schools is Camelback High School in Phoenix. Whenever administrators or teachers suspect that a student has a substance abuse problem, they refer him or her to the school's Teen AA facilitators.

"The beauty of this group," says Susan Patalano, one of the facilitators, "is people have to want to be in it, and it's not a punishment. It's a support." The Teen AA group meets every Thursday; although each meeting is facilitated by an adult, it is the teens who take charge and run the meeting. Patalano says that although measuring success is challenging, she has no doubt that the Teen AA program changes lives for the better. "We plant a lot of seeds, and we never know exactly when they're going to blossom," she says. "But they do."[71]

Hope for the Future

Throughout the years numerous programs have been created in an effort to curtail the persistent problem of drug and alcohol abuse among teens in the United States. Some of these have worked well, while others have been less effective. Because it is a highly complex problem for which there are no simple solutions, even the best initiatives are unlikely to completely end teen substance abuse.

Primary Source Quotes*

What Can Be Done About Teen Substance Abuse?

> **Raising the legal drinking age saved lives.**

—Nicholas Kardaras, "Teen Binge Drinking—the Real American Pastime?," Fox News October 25, 2013. www.foxnews.com.

Kardaras is a New York psychologist who specializes in substance abuse and addiction.

....

> **What this cruel 1984 law did is deprive young people of safe spaces where they could happily drink cheap beer, socialize, chat and flirt in a free but controlled public environment.**

—Camille Paglia, "The Drinking Age Is Past Its Prime," Time, April 23, 2014. http://time.com.

Paglia is a professor at the University of the Arts in Philadelphia, Pennsylvania.

....

Bracketed quotes indicate conflicting positions.

* Editor's Note: While the definition of a primary source can be narrowly or broadly defined, for the purposes of Compact Research, a primary source consists of: 1) results of original research presented by an organization or researcher; 2) eyewitness accounts of events, personal experience, or work experience; 3) first-person editorials offering pundits' opinions; 4) government officials presenting political plans and/or policies; 5) representatives of organizations presenting testimony or policy.

66 It is important to teach parents, administrators, and teachers about signs of illicit drug use, so that adolescents using drugs can be identified and offered treatment. 99

—David Murphey, Megan Barry, Brigitte Vaughn, Lina Guzman, and Mary Terzian, "Use of Illicit Drugs," *Adolescent Health Highlight*, Child Trends, September 2013. www.childtrends.org.

Murphey, Barry, Vaughn, Guzman, and Terzian are mental health professionals with the nonprofit research center Child Trends.

66 Exposing teens to addiction counseling and treatment may actually make what is relatively harmless occasional usage much, much worse. 99

—St. Jude Retreats, "The Drug Use Hysteria and Raising a Teen," Teenlife.com, May 9, 2014. www.teenlife.com.

St. Jude Retreats is an alternative substance abuse treatment program that concentrates on self-directed positive and permanent change.

66 Historically the focus with adolescents has tended to be on steering young people clear of drugs before problems arise. But the reality is that different interventions are needed for adolescents at different places along the substance abuse spectrum, and some require treatment, not just prevention. 99

—Nora D. Volkow, "From the Director," National Institute on Drug Abuse, "Principles of Adolescent Substance Use Disorder Treatment: A Research-Based Guide," January 17, 2014. www.drugabuse.gov.

Volkow is director of the NIDA.

66 Parents must take a zero tolerance when it comes to their child using performance-enhancing drugs. If you take drugs, you quit the team. 99

—David Sortino, "Teen Athletes and Performance-Enhancing Drugs," *Santa Rosa Press Democrat*, August 13, 2013. http://davidsortino.blogs.pressdemocrat.com.

Sortino is a clinical psychologist from northern California.

66 **We have to have better partnerships with the pharmaceutical industries that manufacture these drugs, and we have to appeal to state legislatures to create safety barriers to help control teen drug abuse.** 99

—Manny Alvarez, "Teen Drug Abuse Becoming an Epidemic, Must Be Addressed," *Fox News*, March 14, 2014, www.foxnews.com.

Alvarez is a physician and senior managing health editor for Fox News.

66 **Combating drug abuse is far more complicated than simply attempting to teach our children to 'just say no.'** 99

—Deborah A. Berberich, *Out of the Rabbit Hole: Breaking the Cycle of Addiction*. Bloomington, IN: Xlibris, 2013, p. 11.

Berberich is a clinical psychologist from Southern California who specializes in the treatment of addiction and mental illness.

66 **Programs that work take into account the importance of behavioral norms: they emphasize to students that substance use is not especially common and thereby attempt to counteract the misconception that abstaining from drugs makes a person an oddball.** 99

—Scott O. Lilienfeld and Hal Arkowitz, "Why 'Just Say No' Doesn't Work," *Scientific American*, December 19, 2013. www.scientificamerican.com.

Lilienfeld is a psychology professor at Emory University, and Arkowitz is an associate professor of psychology at the University of Arizona.

66 **Parental expectations, particularly expressing strong disapproval of substance abuse, can be a decisive factor in their teens' behavior.** 99

—Joseph A. Califano Jr., "Accompanying Statement," National Survey on American Attitudes on Substance Abuse XVII: Teens, August 2012. www.casacolumbia.org.

Califano is founder and former chairman of the National Center on Addiction and Substance Abuse at Columbia University.

What Can Be Done About Teen Substance Abuse?

- A long-term study of **11,000 teenagers**, which was conducted by researchers from Duke and Pennsylvania State Universities and released in February 2014, found that pairing school-based substance abuse prevention programs with home-based intervention resulted in a **10 percent decrease** in substance abuse rates.

- In a 2014 study to address the perception that marijuana legalization leads to increased use, economists Daniel Rees, Benjamin Hansen, and D. Mark Anderson found that there was no evidence to support such a causal relationship.

- In a 2014 study that examined how parenting styles influence teenage use of alcohol, tobacco, and marijuana, the European Institute of Studies on Prevention found that the extremes of overly permissive and authoritarian parenting styles were both associated with higher substance use among teens when compared with parenting that encourages a close, affectionate relationship.

- During 2014 the US government allocated **$84 million** in grants to fund community coalition efforts that help prevent and reduce youth substance use.

Attending Religious Services a Strong Protective Factor

There is no magic formula for deterring teens from drinking or using drugs, but experts say there are certain conditions and characteristics that make substance abuse less likely. One of these protective factors is regular attendance at religious services. According to a 2012 study by the National Center on Addiction and Substance Abuse at Columbia University (CASAColumbia), higher religious service attendance corresponded with lower prevalence of tobacco, alcohol, and marijuana use.

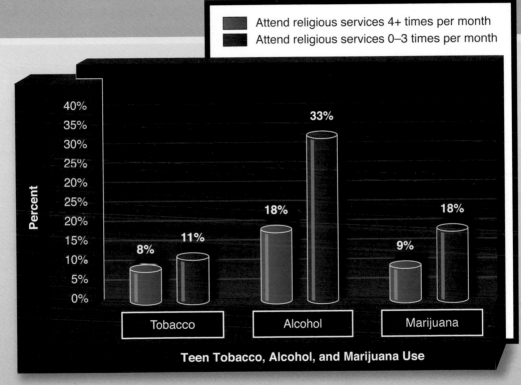

Teen Tobacco, Alcohol, and Marijuana Use

Source: National Center on Addiction and Substance Abuse at Columbia University, National Survey on American Attitudes on Substance Abuse XVII: Teens," August 2012. www.casacolumbia.org.

- In a study published in July 2014 by Partnership for Drug-Free Kids and MetLife Foundation, **34 percent of parents** said they believe there is little they can do to prevent their kids from trying drugs other than alcohol, and **23 percent** felt uncomfortable telling their child not to use drugs because of their own history of drug use.

Parental Rules Matter

Teens may get irritated when their parents establish rules and set limits on what they can do, yet surveys consistently show that young people really do want guidance and rules from their parents. This was evident in a 2013 youth survey conducted by Pennsylvania officials, which found a strong link between the choices teens made about drinking and their parents' rules about alcohol and drug use.

Youth Alcohol Use by Perceived Parental Rules:

Students who reported use within the substance category in relation to responding to the statement "My family has clear rules about alcohol and drug use."

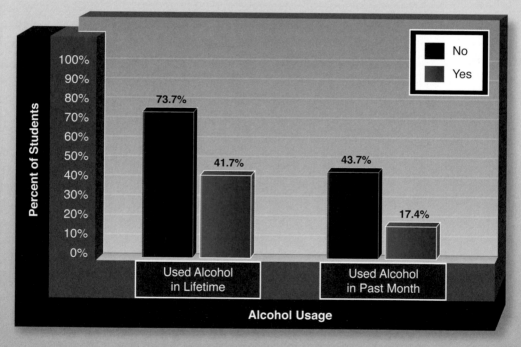

Source: Pennsylvania Commission on Crime and Delinquency, Pennsylvania Department of Drug and Alcohol Programs, and Pennsylvania Department of Education, "Pennsylvania Youth Survey State Report 2013," June 2014. www.pccd.pa.gov.

- According to the antidrug group DoSomething.org, teens who consistently learn about the risks of drugs from their parents are **up to 50 percent** less likely to use drugs than those who do not.

Increased Federal Funding for Substance Abuse Prevention and Treatment

Each year an enormous sum of money is allocated by the federal government for substance abuse prevention and treatment programs. As shown here, the amount for fiscal year 2015 is nearly $11 billion. Although this budget covers programs for people of all ages, many are targeted specifically toward youth substance abuse.

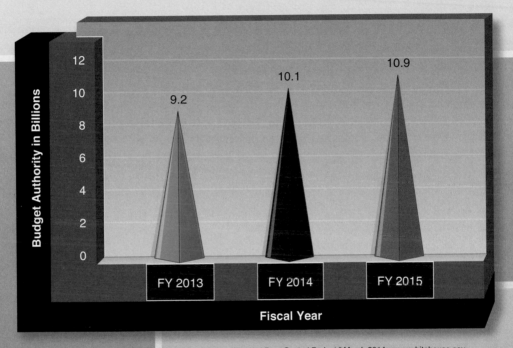

Source: White House Office of National Drug Control Policy, "National Drug Control Budget," March 2014. www.whitehouse.gov.

- A 2013 study by researchers from Iowa State University found that young adults who participated in community-based prevention programs as middle schoolers were **up to 65 percent** less likely to abuse prescription drugs than their peers who did not take part in such programs.

- According to the Partnership for Drug-Free Kids, young people who learn a lot from their parents about the risks of drugs are **up to 50 percent** less likely to use drugs.

Key People and Advocacy Groups

Drug Enforcement Administration (DEA): The United States' leading law enforcement agency for combating the sale and distribution of narcotics and other illegal drugs.

Foundation for a Drug-Free World: A nonprofit organization that provides factual information about drugs to youth and adults to help them make informed decisions and live drug free.

Richard A. Glennon: A medicinal chemist who created synthetic cathinones for research purposes.

Tyler Hamilton: A former Olympic cyclist and gold medal winner who was stripped of his medal for doping; today he shares that experience with teens in an effort to dissuade them from taking performance-enhancing drugs.

John W. Huffman: An organic chemist who created synthetic cannabinoids only for research purposes.

National Center on Addiction and Substance Abuse at Columbia University (CASAColumbia): An organization that focuses on developing effective solutions to address addiction, while reducing the risks associated with substance use.

National Institute on Drug Abuse: A federal agency that supports research efforts and ensures the rapid dissemination of research to improve drug abuse prevention, treatment, and policy.

Partnership for Drug-Free Kids: An organization that helps parents and families solve the problem of teen substance abuse.

Alexander Shulgin: A chemist who resynthesized the drug 3,4-methylenedioxy-methamphetamine (MDMA) and later became known as the father of MDMA.

Substance Abuse and Mental Health Services Administration (SAMHSA): A federal agency whose mission is to reduce the impact of substance abuse and mental illness on America's communities.

Nora D. Volkow: A neuroscientist who serves as director of the National Institute on Drug Abuse (NIDA).

Chronology

1969
Maine and Nebraska lower the legal drinking age from twenty-one to twenty. Within six years more than thirty-five other states also lower their drinking age.

1974
The National Institute on Drug Abuse (NIDA) is established as the lead federal agency to improve public understanding, treatment, and prevention of drug abuse and addiction.

1983
In a collaborative effort, Los Angeles, California, police chief Daryl Gates and the Los Angeles Unified School District launch the Drug Abuse Resistance Education (D.A.R.E.) substance abuse prevention program.

1984
The US Congress passes the National Minimum Drinking Age Act, which motivates states to set the legal drinking age at twenty-one by withholding federal highway funds from those that do not.

1970   **1980**   **1990**

1976
After synthesizing the psychoactive drug MDMA in his backyard laboratory, chemist Alexander T. Shulgin tries it on himself and records the experience in his journal.

1985
The "Just Say No" antidrug campaign, conceived by First Lady Nancy Reagan and targeted at children and teens, is formally launched.

1975
University of Michigan's Institute of Social Justice conducts the first Monitoring the Future survey for the NIDA; more than sixteen thousand high school seniors participate.

1989
In a nationally televised address, President George H.W. Bush declares a renewed effort in the war on drugs and establishes a new agency called the Office of National Drug Control Policy.

1971
President Richard M. Nixon declares a war on drugs by dramatically increasing the size and power of federal drug control agencies and toughening drug laws.

1991
For the first time, eighth and tenth graders are added to the Monitoring the Future survey, along with high school seniors.

1998

A study funded by the National Institute of Justice finds that the D.A.R.E. substance abuse prevention program is not effective at reducing drug abuse among youth.

2011

A study by the Substance Abuse and Mental Health Services Administration (SAMHSA) finds that during the previous year, more than one-fourth of American adolescents drank alcohol and about one-fifth used an illicit drug.

2014

The NIDA's annual Monitoring the Future survey finds that the use of alcohol, cigarettes, prescription pain drugs, and synthetic drugs has declined among teens in the United States; the use of steroids, marijuana, and several other illicit drugs, remains relatively stable.

2006

The US Congress enacts the Sober Truth on Preventing Underage Drinking (STOP) Act, which authorizes $18 million in federal funds to combat underage drinking.

2000

2010

2003

The National Institute on Drug Abuse launches its "NIDA Goes Back to School" drug awareness campaign for teens, parents, and teachers; one feature is the NIDA for Teens website.

2013

Organizers of New York City's annual Electric Zoo Music Festival cancel the third and final day of the event after two concertgoers die and four others become critically ill from overdosing on the psychoactive drug Molly.

2008

A poll by Sacred Heart University in Fairfield, Connecticut, finds that 60 percent of Americans favor drug testing for high school athletes, and 68 percent favor such testing for college athletes.

2009

The annual Monitoring the Future survey finds that 71.9 percent of twelfth graders admitted using alcohol at least once during the previous year, compared with just 2.2 percent who had used steroids.

2015

After Colorado middle schools experience a 24 percent jump in drug-related incidents, substance abuse experts attribute it to the impact of the state's marijuana legalization.

Related Organizations

American Academy of Pediatrics (AAAP)
141 Northwest Point Blvd.
Elk Grove Village, IL 60007-1098
phone: (847) 434-4000; toll-free: (800) 433-9016
fax: (847) 434-8000

An organization of sixty-two thousand pediatricians, the AAAP is committed to the physical, mental, and social health and well-being for all infants, children, adolescents, and young adults. Its website links to a separate HealthyChildren site, where a search engine produces numerous articles related to teen substance abuse.

Community Anti-Drug Coalitions of America (CADCA)
625 Slaters Ln., Suite 300
Alexandria, VA 22314
phone: (800) 542-2322 • fax (703) 706-0565
website: www.cadca.org

Through its network of more than five thousand local coalitions, the CADCA brings together community leaders to address a variety of issues from underage drinking to prescription drug abuse. The website's offerings include a Resources & Research section, an Interactive Media section, and a search engine that produces a number of articles about teen substance abuse.

Drug Enforcement Administration (DEA)
8701 Morrissette Dr.
Springfield, VA 22152
phone: (202) 307-1000
website: www.dea.gov • teen website: www.justthinktwice.com

An agency of the US Department of Justice, the DEA is the United States' leading law enforcement agency for combating the sale and distribution of narcotics and other illegal drugs. Its "Just Think Twice" website is especially for teens and offers a wealth of information about teen substance abuse including fact sheets, news articles, statistics, and true stories.

Drug Free America Foundation

5999 Central Ave., Suite 301
Saint Petersburg, FL 33710
phone: (727) 828-0211 • fax: (727) 828-0212
e-mail: webmaster@dfaf.org • website: www.dfaf.org

The Drug Free America Foundation is a drug prevention and policy organization devoted to reducing drug abuse and drug addiction. Its website has a research section where numerous publications about substance abuse can be found, and a search engine produces additional articles specifically related to young people.

Drug Policy Alliance

131 W. Thirty-Third St., 15th Floor
New York, NY 10001
phone: (212) 613-8020 • fax: (212) 613-8021
e-mail: nyc@drugpolicy.org • website: www.drugpolicy.org

The Drug Policy Alliance promotes alternatives to current drug policy that are grounded in science, compassion, health, and human rights. Its website features drug facts, statistics, information about drug laws and individual rights, and a search engine that produces numerous articles about drug abuse and addiction.

Foundation for a Drug-Free World

1626 N. Wilcox Ave., Suite 1297
Los Angeles, CA 90028
phone: (818) 952-5260; toll-free: (888) 668-6378
e-mail: info@drugfreeworld.org • website: www.drugfreeworld.org

Foundation for a Drug-Free World is a nonprofit organization that provides factual information about drugs to youth and adults to help them make informed decisions and live drug free. A wealth of information is available on the interactive website, including videos, fact sheets, educational booklets, and personal stories of young people who have battled addiction.

National Center on Addiction and Substance Abuse at Columbia University (CASAColumbia)

633 Third Ave., 19th Floor
New York, NY 10017-6706

phone: (212) 841-5200 • fax: (212) 956-8020

e-mail: info@casacolumbia.org • website: www.casacolumbia.org

CASAColumbia is committed to understanding the science of addiction and its implications for health care, public policy, and public education. The organization's website offers numerous materials about substance abuse and addiction, and a search engine produces articles specifically about teen substance abuse.

National Council on Alcoholism and Drug Dependence (NCADD)

217 Broadway, Suite 712

New York, NY 10007

phone: (212) 269-7797 • fax: (212) 269-7510

website: https://ncadd.org

The NCADD is dedicated to fighting alcoholism and drug addiction to alleviate the effects of alcohol and drugs on individuals, families, and communities. Its website offers extensive information about substance abuse as well as a separate For Youth section designed especially for young people who have questions about substance abuse.

National Institute on Alcohol Abuse and Alcoholism (NIAAA)

5635 Fishers Ln., MSC 9304

Bethesda, MD 20892-9304

phone: (301) 443-3860

e-mail: niaaaweb-r@exchange.nih.gov • website: www.niaaa.nih.gov

An agency of the National Institutes of Health, the NIAAA is the lead federal agency for research on alcohol use and abuse. Its website features brochures, research updates, news articles, fact sheets, classroom resources, and videocasts.

National Institute on Drug Abuse (NIDA)

National Institutes of Health

6001 Executive Blvd., Room 5213

Bethesda, MD 20892-9561

phone: (301) 443-1124

e-mail: information@nida.nih.gov • website: www.drugabuse.gov

The NIDA supports research efforts and ensures the rapid dissemination of research to improve drug abuse prevention, treatment, and policy. The website links to a separate "NIDA for Teens" site, which is designed especially for young people and provides a wealth of information about illicit drugs, drug abuse, and addiction.

Office of Adolescent Health (OAH)
1101 Wootton Pkwy., Suite 700
Rockville, MD 20852
phone: (240) 453-2846
e-mail: oah.gov@hhs.gov • website: www.hhs.gov/ash/oah

An agency of the US Department of Health and Human Services, the OAH is dedicated to improving the health and well-being of adolescents. Its website has an Adolescent Health section that contains a wide variety of articles, fact sheets, and other information specifically for teens about health and nutrition, mental health, and substance abuse.

Partnership for Drug-Free Kids (formerly Partnership at DrugFree.org)
352 Park Ave. South, 9th Floor
New York, NY 10010
phone: (212) 922-1560 • fax: (212) 922-1570
website: www.drugfree.org

The Partnership for Drug-Free Kids is dedicated to helping parents and families solve the problem of teenage substance abuse. A large number of informative publications about teen substance abuse can be accessed through the website search engine.

Substance Abuse and Mental Health Services Administration (SAMHSA)
1 Choke Cherry Rd.
Rockville, MD 20857
phone: (877) 726-4727 • fax: (240) 221-4292
e-mail: SAMHSAInfo@samhsa.hhs.gov • website: www.samhsa.gov

The SAMHSA's mission is to reduce the impact of substance abuse and mental illness on America's communities. The site offers a wealth of information about substance abuse, including teen substance abuse, and numerous publications are available through its search engine.

For Further Research

Books

Taite Adams, *Opiate Addiction: The Painkiller Addiction Epidemic, Heroin Addiction and the Way Out*. St. Petersburg, FL: Rapid Response, 2013.

Marc Aronoff, *One Toke: A Survival Guide for Teens*. Lenox, MA: Porter House, 2014.

Sheri Mabry Bestor, *Substance Abuse: The Ultimate Teen Guide*. Lanham, MD: Scarecrow, 2013.

Mark J. Estren, *Prescription Drug Abuse*. Oakland, CA: Ronin, 2013.

Periodicals

Victoria Bekiempis, "Is Teen Drinking Worse than Teen Marijuana Use?," *Newsweek*, September 2, 2014.

Michael Blanding, "There's Something About Molly," *Boston Globe*, January 26, 2014.

Julie Bogen, "What You Need to Know About Molly," *Teen Vogue*, September 2013.

John DiConsiglio, "I Was Hooked on Prescription Drugs," *Scholastic Choices*, January 2012.

Eliza Gray, "The Rise of Fake Pot," *Time*, April 21, 2014.

Christopher Ingraham, "Study: Teens Who Smoke Weed Daily Are 60% Less Likely to Complete High School than Those Who Never Use," *Washington Post*, September 9, 2014.

Sharon Jayson, "Pot Studies Suggest Regular Use Is Bad for Teen Brains," *USA Today*, August 9, 2014.

Elizabeth Foy Larsen, "Good Teens Turned Drug Addicts," *Scholastic Choices*, October 2014.

Meredith Matthews, "Bitter Pill: Ecstasy Is a Club You Don't Want to Join," *Current Health Teens*, a *Weekly Reader* publication, March 2012.

Dustin Racioppi, "Old Drug Making a Comeback as 'Molly,'" *USA Today*, January 2, 2014.

Julia Rubin, "How Heroin Is Invading America's Schools," *Teen Vogue*, September 2013.

Julie Scelfo, "Just Say No, Yes or Maybe," *New York Times*, October 29, 2014.

Alice G. Walton, "Why Synthetic Marijuana Is More Toxic to the Brain than Pot," *Forbes*, August 28, 2014.

Internet Sources

Greg Campbell, "Colorado Teens Smoking Less Pot Since Legalization," *Daily Caller*, August 8, 2014. http://dailycaller.com/2014/08/08/colorado-teens-smoking-less-pot-since-legalization.

Joette Giovinco, "Binge Drinking Takes Teen to the Brink of Death," Fox News, April 28, 2014. www.myfoxtampabay.com/story/2487 3908/2014/03/03/binge-drinking-took-teen-to-the-brink-of-death.

Drew Griffin and Nelli Black, "Deadly High: How Synthetic Drugs Are Killing Kids," CNN, December 2, 2014. www.cnn.com/2014/12/01/us/synthetic-drugs-investigation.

Anne Harding, "Blackouts Common Among Teen Drinkers, Study Finds," Live Science, December 16, 2014. www.livescience.com/49155-blackouts-teen-drinking.html.

Rima Himelstein, "Teen Heroin Use: An Unfortunate Reality," Philly. com *Healthy Kids* (blog), September 10, 2013. www.philly.com/philly/blogs/healthy_kids/Teen-heroin-use-an-unfortunate-reality.html.

Alan Mozes, "Prescription Drug Abuse Up Among U.S. Teens: Survey," HealthDay, April 23, 2013. http://consumer.healthday.com/general-health-information-16/drug-abuse-news-210/prescription-drug-abuse-up-among-u-s-teens-survey-675654.html.

Kristi Ramsay, "Agonized Parents Make a Plea: Beware the Dangers of Synthetic Drugs," CNN, December 2, 2014. www.cnn.com/2014/12/01/us/synthetic-drugs-parents.

Source Notes

Overview

1. Taylor Snider, "The Dangers of Molly," recorded interview, CKNW, October 3, 2014. www.cknw.com.
2. Taylor Snider, post on Facebook, September 24, 2014. www.facebook.com.
3. Snider, post on Facebook.
4. Go Ask Alice, "When Ecstasy Is No Longer Ecstasy: Coming Down," Columbia University, December 13, 2013. http://goaskalice.columbia.edu.
5. Quoted in Donna Leinwand Leger, "Overdoses Attributed to Club Drug 'Molly' Increase," *USA Today*, September 25, 2013. www.usatoday.com.
6. Nora Volkow, "From the Director," in National Institute on Drug Abuse, "Inhalants," July 2012. www.drugabuse.gov.
7. Michele Leonhart, testimony before the United States House of Representatives Committee on Appropriations, Subcommittee on Commerce, Justice, Science and Related Agencies, April 12, 2014. www.erowid.org.
8. Quoted in Brian Alexander, "'This Is Not a Game': After Son's Death, Parents Warn About Synthetic Pot," Health, *Today*, August 14, 2014. www.today.com.
9. National Institute on Drug Abuse, "DrugFacts: High School and Youth Trends," December 2014. www.drugabuse.gov.
10. National Institute on Drug Abuse, "What to Do If Your Teen or Young Adult Has a Problem with Drugs." www.drugabuse.gov.
11. Suzanne Kane, "Signs of Pot Use in Teens, from Breath Mints to Burns," Elements Behavioral Health, August 5, 2013. www.elementsbehavioralhealth.com.
12. Kane, "Signs of Pot Use in Teens, from Breath Mints to Burns."
13. Federal Trade Commission, "Stopping Teens' Easy Access to Alcohol," September 2013. www.consumer.ftc.gov.
14. Carole Cadwalladr, "How I Bought Drugs from 'Dark Net'—It's Just Like Amazon Run by Cartels," *Guardian*, October 5, 2013. www.theguardian.com.
15. Mayo Clinic, "Teen Drug Abuse: Help Your Teen Avoid Drugs," January 12, 2013. www.mayoclinic.org.
16. Will, "Trying to Fit In Leads to a Life of Addiction," Narconon International. www.narconon.org.
17. Patricia Cavazos-Rehg, Melissa Krauss, Richard Grucza, and Laura Bierut, "Characterizing the Followers and Tweets of a Marijuana-Focused Twitter Handle," *Journal of Medical Internet Research*, June 27, 2014. www.jmir.org.
18. David Murphey, Megan Barry, Brigitte Vaughn, Lina Guzman, and Mary Terzian, "Adolescent Health Highlight: Use of Illicit Drugs," *Adolescent Health Highlight*, Child Trends, September 2013. www.childtrends.org.
19. National Institute on Drug Abuse, "Principles of Adolescent Substance Use Disorder Treatment: A Research-Based Guide," January 17, 2014. www.drugabuse.gov.
20. Quoted in Fox News, "Study Finds Many Parents Underestimate Dangers of Teens Abusing Prescription Drugs," April 23, 2013. www.foxnews.com.

21. Office of Adolescent Health, "Illicit and Nonillicit Drug Use," December 31, 2014. www.hhs.gov.

22. Quoted in Evan Allen, "Father of Molly Victim Speaks to Students About Its Dangers," *Boston Globe*, January 26, 2015. www.bostonglobe.com.

How Serious a Problem Is Substance Abuse Among Teens?

23. Lloyd D. Johnston, interview by Deborah Holdship, "Monitoring the Future," *Michigan Today*, January 21, 2015. http://michigantoday.umich.edu.

24. Quoted in Jared Wadley, "Use of Alcohol, Cigarettes, and a Number of Illicit Drugs Declines Among U.S. Teens," University of Michigan News, December 16, 2014. http://monitoringthefuture.org.

25. Child Trends, "Binge Drinking," August 2014. www.childtrends.org.

26. Quoted in Melissa Pandika, "Extreme Binge Drinking Common Among High School Seniors, Study Finds," *Los Angeles Times*, September 16, 2013. www.latimes.com.

27. National Institute on Alcohol Abuse and Alcoholism, "College Drinking," July 2013. http://pubs.niaaa.nih.gov.

28. Philip J. Hanlon, "Prepared Remarks by Philip J. Hanlon, President of Dartmouth College," *Washington Post*, April 16, 2014. www.washingtonpost.com.

29. National Institute on Drug Abuse, "Spice ('Synthetic Marijuana')," DrugFacts, December 2012. www.drugabuse.gov.

30. Quoted in Kristi Ramsay, "Agonized Parents Make a Plea: Beware the Dangers of Synthetic Drugs," CNN, December 2, 2014. www.cnn.com.

31. Quoted in Eliza Gray, "The Rise of Fake Pot," *Time*, April 14, 2014. www.klobuchar.senate.gov.

32. Quoted in Gray, "The Rise of Fake Pot."

33. Gray, "The Rise of Fake Pot."

34. Quoted in Associated Press, "Survey: Teen HGH Use Is On the Rise," ESPN, July 23, 2014. http://espn.go.com.

35. Quoted in Associated Press, "Survey: Teen HGH Use Is On the Rise."

36. Community Anti-Drug Coalitions of America, "Alarming Stats About American Indian Youth Substance Abuse a 'Wake-Up Call' Says NIDA's Dr. Volkow," September 25, 2014. www.cadca.org.

37. Quoted in Sherri Kuhn, "Why LGBT Teens Are Turning to Drugs," SheKnows, July 11, 2014. www.sheknows.com.

Why Do Teens Use Alcohol and Drugs?

38. Promises Treatment Centers, "10 Reasons Teens Abuse Alcohol or Drugs," October 24, 2013. www.promises.com.

39. Elements Behavioral Health, "Impact of Alcoholic Parents on Teens with Substance Abuse Problems," June 22, 2013. www.elementsbehavioralhealth.com.

40. Alan Schwarz, "Risky Rise of the Good-Grade Pill," *New York Times*, June 9, 2012. www.nytimes.com.

41. Schwarz, "Risky Rise of the Good-Grade Pill."

42. Lloyd D. Johnston, Patrick M. O'Malley, Richard A. Miech, Jerald G. Bachman, and John E. Schulenberg, "Monitoring the Future: 2014 Overview," February 2015. http://monitoringthefuture.org.

43. Evie Blad, "Teens Overestimate Peers' Involvement in Risky Behaviors, Study Finds," *Education Week*, January 7, 2015. http://blogs.edweek.org.

44. American Academy of Child & Adolescent Psychiatry, "The Teen Brain: Behavior, Problem Solving, and Decision Making," Facts for Families, December 2011. www.aacap.org.

45. Nora D. Volkow, "Brain in Progress: Why Teens Can't Always Resist Temptation," *TEDMED blog*, January 27, 2015. http://blog.tedmed.com.

46. Volkow, "Brain in Progress."

47. Quoted in Megan Brooks, "Biomarker of Future Alcohol Abuse Risk in Teens?," Medscape Medical News, November 18, 2014. www.medscape.com.

What Are the Consequences of Substance Abuse?

48. Quoted in Kristi Ramsay, "Agonized Parents Make a Plea: Beware the Dangers of Synthetic Drugs," CNN, December 2, 2014. www.cnn.com.

49. Quoted in Anna Schecter, "Taxpayer Money Created 'Legal Marijuana' Used by Teens," ABC News, June 6, 2011. http://abcnews.go.com.

50. Quoted in Schecter, "Taxpayer Money Created 'Legal Marijuana' Used by Teens."

51. Quoted in Greg Allen, "Florida Bans Cocaine-Like 'Bath Salts' Sold in Stores," NPR, February 8, 2011. www.npr.org.

52. Quoted in Virginia Commonwealth University, "Dangerous Designer Drug Packs a One-Two Punch," March 14, 2013. www.cctr.vcu.edu.

53. Foundation for a Drug-Free World, "The Truth About Alcohol." www.drugfreeworld.org.

54. Roxanne Dryden-Edwards, "What Is Alcohol Poisoning?," MedicineNet, March 12, 2014. www.medicinenet.com.

55. Quoted in Joette Giovinco, "Binge Drinking Takes Teen to the Brink of Death," Fox News, April 28, 2014. www.myfoxtampabay.com.

56. Quoted in Giovinco, "Binge Drinking Takes Teen to the Brink of Death."

57. Paul, "The Truth About Marijuana," Foundation for a Drug-Free World. www.drugfreeworld.org.

58. American College of Pediatricians, "Marijuana Use: Detrimental to Youth," October 2014. www.acpeds.org.

59. American College of Pediatricians, "Marijuana Use: Detrimental to Youth."

What Can Be Done About Teen Substance Abuse?

60. Quoted in Laila Kearney, "U.S. Schools Turn to New Programs to Warn Teens of Drug Risks," Reuters, February 6, 2015. www.reuters.com.

61. Quoted in Rose Quinn, "Delco Experts, Families Talk About Heroin Horrors," *Delaware County Daily Times*, February 8, 2015. www.nopetaskforce.org.

62. Quoted in Quinn, "Delco Experts, Families Talk About Heroin Horrors."

63. Elements Behavioral Health, "The Above the Influence Teen Drug Campaign—Helping Kids Avoid Alcohol and Drugs," *Addiction Treatment Magazine*, November 12, 2013. www.addictiontreatmentmagazine.com.

64. Elements Behavioral Health, "The Above the Influence Teen Drug Campaign."
65. Above the Influence, February 11, 2015. http://abovetheinfluence.tumblr.com.
66. Quoted in Neal Wagner, "Above the Influence Takes Hold in Schools," *Shelby County Reporter*, January 17, 2013. www.shelbycountyreporter.com.
67. Partnership for Drug-Free Kids, "Who's the Most Powerful Influence in Your Child's Life? You," 2015. www.drugfree.org.
68. Joseph A. Califano, "Accompanying Statement," National Survey on American Attitudes on Substance Abuse XVII: Teens, August 2012. www.casacolumbia.org.
69. Califano, "Accompanying Statement," National Survey on American Attitudes on Substance Abuse XVII: Teens.
70. Murphey et al., "Use of Illicit Drugs."
71. Quoted in Vivian Padilla, "Arizona Worst or Close in CDC Measures of Teen Substance Abuse," Cronkite News, May 2, 2014. http://cronkitenewsonline.com.

List of Illustrations

List of Illustrations

Index

Note: Boldface page numbers indicate illustrations.